IS THERE A BERMUDA TRIANGLE?
Science and Sea Mysteries

With all of the sensationalism surrounding this subject, it is important that a reasoned account of this region and the unusual happenings that have occurred there be reported. This is just what *Is There a Bermuda Triangle?* does. Along with recreating the mysterious ship and airplane disappearances, the author explains the meteorologic and oceanographic peculiarities of this part of the North Atlantic, which can provide a general accounting for most of these losses. He shows the potential links between these phenomena and the unexplained disappearances. Phenomena peculiar to the region include a circular system of ocean currents that outline and entrap the Sargasso Sea, nocturnal storms that develop with explosive suddenness and disappear just as quickly, waterspouts, wandering eddy currents, severe underwater turbulence, and frequent local disturbances of the earth's magnetic field. A look into the oceanographic and atmospheric research program experiments going on in the area shows that with increased scientific knowledge, the mysteries of the area may become less mysterious. This rigorous scientific treatment of the Bermuda Triangle phenomena is a welcome—and needed—addition to the existing literature.

Is There a Bermuda Triangle?

SCIENCE and SEA MYSTERIES

Michael J. Cusack

photographs - maps

Julian Messner
New York

Published by Julian Messner, a Division of
Simon & Schuster, Inc.
1 West 39 Street, New York, N. Y. 10018.

Library of Congress Cataloging in Publication Data

Cusack, Michael J
Is there a Bermuda Triangle?

Bibliography: p. 120
Includes index.
SUMMARY: Recreates some famous ship and plane disappearances explaining most of them meteorologically and oceanographically.
1. Bermuda Triangle—Juvenile literature.
[1. Bermuda Triangle] I. Title.
G525.C963 910'.09'16363 76-2717
ISBN 0-671-32782-8
ISBN 0-671-32783-6 lib. bdg.

Printed in the United States of America

To all the people who asked the question.

CONTENTS

ACKNOWLEDGMENTS

For permission to excerpt and reprint copyrighted material in this book, the author and publisher are grateful to the following:

Bantam Books, Inc.
for excerpt from *The Devil's Triangle* by Richard Winer. Copyright © 1974 by Bantam Books, Inc.
Harper & Row, Publishers, Inc.
for excerpt from *The Bermuda Triangle Mystery—Solved* by Lawrence David Kusche. Copyright © 1975 by Lawrence David Kusche.
Lombard Associates, Inc.
for excerpt from *The Riddle of the Bermuda Triangle,* edited by Martin Ebon. Published by The New American Library. Copyright © 1975 Lombard Associates.

Chapter I

FLIGHT 19 IS MISSING!

It was about ten minutes past two on the afternoon of December 5, 1945. The sky over the U.S. Naval Air Station at Fort Lauderdale, Florida, was fairly clear. The wind was brisk. And the sound of airplane engines filled the air.

One by one, five clumsy-looking, single-engine aircraft roared down the Naval Air Station runway. Climbing toward the sun, the five planes joined formation above the base. Flight 19 was ready to start its training mission.

Flight 19 circled the base and then flew eastward out over the white-flecked waves of the Atlantic Ocean—out into the vast unknown.

One of the great air mysteries of all times had just begun!

Flight 19 never returned. No trace of the planes or their crews was ever found. Although much has been said, written, and argued about the men and planes of Flight 19, their disappearance is still a baffling mystery.

The planes of Flight 19 were U.S. Navy torpedo bombers known as TBM Avengers. These planes were veterans of World War II. So were most of their crewmen.

Navy Lt. Charles C. Taylor, the pilot in charge of Flight 19, was a senior qualified flight instructor with more than a thousand hours flight time. The other four pilots were considered qualified. Each of them had logged between 350 and

400 hours flight time. Furthermore, all five pilots were familiar with the planes they were flying. Each of them had put in at least 55 hours in TBM aircraft.

So, why were they on a training flight?

In the U.S. Navy, as in most other modern armed forces, training is never really over, particularly for air crews. Experienced airmen return again and again to training centers to learn new techniques and to refresh their knowledge of old techniques. That was the case with the men of Flight 19. They were at Fort Lauderdale to study advanced overwater navigation methods and various new uses of TBM aircraft.

On the afternoon of December 5, 1945, Flight 19 was engaged in solving navigation problem No. 1. That problem required Flight 19 to travel eastward from Fort Lauderdale to semisubmerged sandbanks known as Hens and Chickens Shoals. The Shoals are about 56 miles from Fort Lauderdale.

At the Hens and Chickens Shoals, the members of Flight 19 were to practice low-level bombing techniques. Following the bombing practice, Flight 19 was to continue on course to a point 67 miles east of the Shoals. At that point, the flight was scheduled to make a sharp turn and fly northward for a distance of 75 miles. That northerly course would take Flight 19 over Grand Bahama Island. Shortly after passing over the island, the flight was supposed to turn into a west-by-southwest course and fly home to Fort Lauderdale on the final, 120-mile leg of the journey.

However, the training mission for the men of Flight 19 did not work out as planned. Even before the planes left the ground, there was a change in the lineup. Fifteen crewmen were assigned to Flight 19—a pilot, a gunner, and a radio operator for each aircraft. Shortly before takeoff, one man reported in sick and thus missed the mission. There were rumors that other men, including Lt. Taylor, asked to be excused from the flight. Navy records are not clear on this topic. But if crewmen other than the sick person asked to be excused, they were obviously turned down, because Flight 19 left on time with fourteen men aboard the five planes.

As the planes flew eastward from Fort Lauderdale, they appeared to be right on course for the Hens and Chickens Shoals. But no one knows whether Flight 19 reached the Shoals. No one knows how much of navigation problem No. 1 was completed by Flight 19.

For almost an hour and a half, not a word was heard from Flight 19. Then at 3:40 P.M., a puzzling radio message was picked up by Lt. Robert Cox, who was flying over Fort Lauderdale.

On the radio channel used by training flights, Lt. Cox heard an unidentified voice call, "Powers, Powers. What is your compass reading?"

Lt. Cox heard no reply to this question.

After a pause, the question was repeated. This time the unknown caller added, "I don't know where we are. We must have gotten lost after that last turn."

U.S. Navy TBM Avenger Torpedo Bombers. On December 5, 1945, five aircraft of this type flew out over the Atlantic Ocean from Fort Lauderdale, Florida . . . and vanished. (*U.S. Navy*)

With the word "lost" ringing in his ears, Lt. Cox promptly radioed the Fort Lauderdale Naval Air Station and told them that some unidentified planes were lost.

Actually, the planes weren't unidentified. Though Lt. Cox didn't know it at the time, Powers was the name of one of the pilots of Flight 19.

Following his call to Fort Lauderdale, Lt. Cox tried to contact the "unidentified" planes. After several tries, he finally succeeded. He was answered by a pilot using the call sign FT-28.

Since FT-28 was the call sign assigned to Lt. Taylor, the Fort Lauderdale control tower operators became aware that the lost planes were those of Flight 19. From that time on, every effort was made to help the lost pilots.

At the beginning, all contacts with the lost flight were made through Lt. Cox, who continued to fly over Fort Lauderdale.

At about 4:00 P.M., Lt. Cox asked FT-28, ". . . what is your trouble?"

Lt. Taylor replied, "Both my compasses are out. I am trying to find Fort Lauderdale."

Lt. Taylor then added, "I am over land, but it's broken. I'm sure I'm in the Florida Keys, but I don't know how far down and I don't know how to get to Fort Lauderdale."

Lt. Cox told Lt. Taylor to keep the sun on his port (left) wing and fly up the Florida coastline, past Miami, and on to Fort Lauderdale.

Assuming that Flight 19 was coming up from the Florida Keys, Lt. Cox turned his plane southward to meet them. In doing so, Lt. Cox expected the radio signals from FT-28 to become louder and clearer as the gap narrowed between his plane and Flight 19.

But just the opposite happened. As Lt. Cox flew south, the radio messages from FT-28 got fainter and fainter. Finally, they faded out completely.

Lt. Cox concluded that he was having trouble with his radio equipment. So he flew back to Fort Lauderdale and landed at approximately 4:25 P.M.

Before Lt. Cox landed, radio operators at Fort Lauderdale Naval Air Station, at Port Everglades Air Sea Rescue Station, and at a seaplane base near Miami were in off-and-on contact with Flight 19. In addition to receiving faint, and frequently garbled, radio signals from Flight 19, the radio operators also overheard snatches of talk between the pilots of Flight 19.

During these contacts with Flight 19, the Port Everglades operations officers advised Lt. Taylor to put another pilot in charge of the flight. They made this suggestion because Lt. Taylor's compasses were not working, and the officers must have reasoned that a pilot with good compasses could lead the flight homeward.

No reply was heard from Lt. Taylor at that time. But it appears that about an hour later, Lt. Taylor turned over the leadership of the flight to Captain Powers of the U.S. Marine Corps.

From the time it was learned that Flight 19 was lost, radio-direction-finding stations and radar stations along the Florida coast tried to fix the position of Flight 19. But they were not successful.

Overheard scraps of conversation between the pilots of Flight 19 seemed to indicate that the flight was changing course many times. The messages also indicated some confusion and disagreement among the pilots of Flight 19.

"If we would just fly west we would get home," one unidentified pilot said.

Minutes later, another unidentified pilot exclaimed angrily: "We are going too damn far north instead of east."

Finally at 5:15 P.M., Lt. Taylor told Port Everglades operations that Flight 19 was flying west on a 270° heading.

There was a long pause. Then Lt. Taylor announced, "We will fly 270° until we hit the beach or run out of gas."

All of the conversations from and between the pilots of Flight 19 took place over the radio frequency used by training flights. However, that particular radio channel was plagued by static and interference. At various times, the operators at Fort Lauderdale and at the other ground stations asked Lt. Taylor to switch his radio to the emergency frequency.

Lt. Taylor did not respond until 5:54 P.M. At that time, he stated that he would not change channels because he was afraid that he might lose contact with the other pilots of Flight 19. Perhaps the emergency channel was not working on one or more of the radios in the flight.

At last, around 6:00 P.M., a radio-direction-finding station got a rough bearing on Flight 19's position. An approximate fix placed the flight well north of the Bahamas and about sixty miles east of the area of Florida where Cape Kennedy is now located.

That meant that Flight 19 was much farther north and east than Lt. Taylor realized. But for some reason, this information was never given to Flight 19.

The ground operators were not alarmed by that fix. They estimated that each plane in Flight 19 carried enough aviation gasoline to last until 8:00 P.M. And they figured that if Flight 19 were to continue on 270° heading, the planes would pass over the Florida coast with fuel to spare.

However, the pilots of Flight 19 didn't seem to realize that they had fuel to spare. At 6:02 P.M. an unidentified pilot said, "We may have to ditch any minute."

But evidently they didn't ditch at that time. For, at 6:37 P.M., a different pilot asked: "What course are we on now?"

Over the next half hour, ground-based operators overheard garbled snatches of conversation between pilots of Flight 19.

At 7:00 P.M. Port Everglades operators clearly heard a call from one pilot to Lt. Taylor.

"FT-3 calling FT-28. FT-3 calling FT-28."

There was no reply.

The call was repeated a few more times.

And those were the last words heard from Flight 19!

Before those last words were heard, however, a massive air-sea search for the lost flight was begun. Around 6:20 P.M., a seaplane was launched from the Miami area base to search sea and sky north and east of Fort Lauderdale. As time passed, other planes took to the air. Within a few hours, many planes were crisscrossing a wide area ranging from the Florida Keys to Jacksonville and over into the Gulf of Mexico. Ships were also alerted. But darkness soon hampered the search. So did storm clouds and heavy rain in places. And no trace of the men or planes of Flight 19 was found.

Then, a little more than an hour after the last words were heard from Flight 19, another chapter was added to the mystery.

PBM Mariner Flying Boats. While searching for the lost Flight 19, a long-range patrol plane of this type disappeared. (*U.S. Navy*)

One of the search planes vanished without leaving a trace!

The plane was a PBM Martin Mariner flying boat—a long-range patrol aircraft, particularly suited for search and rescue missions. More than one of these flying boats was engaged in the search for Flight 19.

The PBM that disappeared took off from the Banana River (Florida) Naval Air Station at 7:27 P.M. With a crew of thirteen experienced naval airmen aboard, the ill-fated flying boat was scheduled to fly north and then east from Banana River toward the last estimated position of Flight 19.

Shortly after takeoff, the pilot of the PBM reported his position. He was to report his position again and the progress of the search within an hour.

That report never came!

When the PBM did not report on time, Banana River radio operators started calling the plane. Soon, operators at other stations joined in. Other planes started calling. But there was no word from the PBM.

As the minutes ticked by, Navy officials became more and more worried. Could it be that six planes and twenty-seven men had simply vanished somewhere in the Atlantic?

It seemed that way.

Then at 9:10 P.M., naval officials received a possible clue to the fate of the PBM.

When the PBM flew off on its search mission, a merchant ship, the S.S. *Gaines Mills*, was sailing near the Florida coast. At about 7:50 P.M., the ship was forty-five miles east of Banana River when some crewmen on it saw and heard an explosion in the sky. Later the ship passed through an oil slick.

Did that explosion and oil slick mark the death of the PBM?

No one knows for sure. If the plane exploded in the air, surely the sea would have been showered with debris. But no debris was recovered. The S.S. *Gaines Mills* did pass through an oil slick. But oil slicks are not uncommon that close to shore.

For more than a week after the loss of Flight 19 and the PBM, about 100 planes and 20 ships searched a 250,000-mile area. But they found no trace of the missing planes and men.

What could have happened to Flight 19? What could have happened to the PBM flying boat?

Did some violent storm snatch all six planes from the sky?

No major storms were reported in the area at the time. However, there were high winds and heavy rain in places off the Florida coast, particularly in the vicinity of Banana River. But none of the other search planes experienced any great difficulty with the weather except that it reduced search visibility.

Might some act of war have caused the loss of all six aircraft? Were the planes sabotaged? Did someone plant time bombs on them?

An act of sabotage could explain the midair explosion of the PBM, if the PBM did indeed explode in midair. But why would anyone want to sabotage six planes in December, 1945? The United States was not at war at the time. World War II had been over for several months. So that makes an act of war unlikely as the cause of the loss of the PBM and Flight 19.

Could the losses of Flight 19 and of the PBM be unrelated? A Navy board of inquiry felt that the losses of the PBM and of Flight 19 might have separate, unrelated causes.

After considerable investigation, the board of inquiry could not find any definite reasons for the losses of Flight 19 and the PBM. However, the board offered the opinion that Flight 19 became hopelessly lost, and the five planes ditched in the sea after running out of fuel. The board also offered the opinion that the PBM was destroyed by an explosion of unknown origin.

These opinions of the Navy board did not satisfy many

people. Some asked how could experienced pilots become hopelessly lost on such a simple mission? And if the planes were forced to ditch, why were no life rafts, or bodies, or gear found?

Chapter 2

OTHER PLANES VANISH

Since that fateful day in December 1945, the story of the disappearance of Flight 19 and the PBM flying boat has been told and retold. And each retelling seems to make the mystery even more mysterious.

One oft-told tale of the event says that the Fort Lauderdale control tower ordered Flight 19 to fly west. And Lt. Taylor replied, "We don't know which way is west . . . we can't be sure of any direction."

A news bulletin issued by the National Geographic Society in 1967 states that the leader of Flight 19 said: "Everything is wrong . . . strange. We can't be sure of any direction. Even the sea doesn't look as it should."

These "words" of Lt. Taylor do not appear in Navy records. Yet, these "conversations" have been repeated in one form or another in most accounts of the loss of Flight 19. As a result, many people have become convinced that some strange force baffled and bewildered the pilots of Flight 19.

Numerous writers and their readers now believe that "something strange is going on out there" in the Atlantic Ocean east of Florida, south of Bermuda, and north of the West Indies.

Perhaps this feeling of strangeness about that sea area would have faded in time if the TBMs of Flight 19 and the searching PBM had been the only planes to vanish there. But those six planes were not the first—and certainly not the last—aircraft to disappear mysteriously in that area of the Atlantic Ocean.

Before World War II, many a small plane was lost over the stormy Atlantic. But in the days when brave pilots in flimsy planes were pioneering overwater flight, these losses were half-expected.

However, as aircraft, radios, and navigation instruments were improved, plane losses were no longer taken for granted. From the war years on, each loss was bound to cause a stir, a search, and an inquiry. That's exactly what happened when a four-engined Navy bomber disappeared nearly five months before the loss of Flight 19.

On July 18, 1945, a big Navy *Privateer* bomber flew east-

***Santa Maria, Pinta, Nina.* On his first voyage to the New World, Christopher Columbus wrote in his log about strange sights. He found masses of weeds floating on the open sea. He encountered currents that seemed to move his ships against the wind. He saw strange lights on the sea surface. All of these unusual sights were encountered southwest of Bermuda. (*N. Y. Public Library*)**

ward from the Miami Naval Air Station. The plane headed out over the sea—and disappeared. A massive search revealed no trace of the plane or of its fifteen crewmen. An inquiry could find no cause for the loss.

Two years later, another four-engined plane disappeared in the same general area. On the morning of July 3, 1947, a U.S. Air Force C-54 transport plane left Bermuda for West Palm Beach, Florida. In addition to a crew of six men, the plane carried a load of mixed cargo.

The cargo, the crew, and the plane never reached Florida. They disappeared somewhere between Bermuda and the Florida coast. But in this case, the missing plane left a trace. Search planes spotted seat cushions and a few scraps of wreckage floating in the water about 100 miles southwest of Bermuda. From these clues, Air Force investigators figured that the lost C-54 had been ripped apart by a furious storm.

Few other plane disappearances in the Bermuda-Florida area would provide such clues. The next plane disappearance in the area left no telltale wreckage at all.

Early in the morning of January 30, 1948, the pilot of a British South American Airways plane contacted the control tower at Hamilton, Bermuda. The pilot of the *Star Tiger* reported that they were 440 miles northeast of Bermuda. Though the plane was bucking strong head winds, the pilot estimated that they would land at Hamilton within two and a half hours.

No other word was ever heard from the *Star Tiger.* The airliner, with twenty-five passengers and six crew men aboard, never reached Bermuda.

When the airliner failed to land on schedule, search planes and ships started combing a wide area of the Atlantic. But no trace of the *Star Tiger* was ever found. And an inquiry that was held several months later could find no definite cause for the loss of the plane.

One year later, mystery was piled on top of mystery. Another British South American Airways plane disappeared in the vicinity of Bermuda on January 17, 1949. The missing plane was the *Star Ariel*, sister ship of the lost *Star Tiger*.

On the second leg of a flight from London, England, to Santiago, Chile, the *Star Ariel* left Bermuda at 8:42 A.M. on January 17, 1949. The plane's next scheduled stop was Kingston, Jamaica.

An hour after leaving Bermuda, Capt. J. McPhee, pilot of the *Star Ariel*, reported that all was well. The weather was good. The sky was clear. With a strong tail wind boosting them along, the crew of the *Star Ariel* expected to reach Kingston on schedule.

Capt. McPhee told Bermuda flight control that he was changing radio frequency in order to contact Kingston flight control. Bermuda acknowledged the request. But Capt. McPhee did not contact Kingston. Following the 9:42 A.M. position report to Bermuda, the *Star Ariel* made no further contact with any station.

But it wasn't until around 2:00 in the afternoon, shortly before *Star Ariel* was due to land at Kingston, that anyone realized that the airliner had been out of contact with all stations for hours. Up to that time, flight controllers at Kingston thought the airliner was in contact with Bermuda. And flight controllers at Bermuda thought. . . .

When it was finally learned that *Star Ariel* had not been in touch with anyone since 9:42 A.M., frenzied attempts were made to reach the plane. All of those efforts were in vain. It soon became obvious that *Star Ariel* was overdue and missing.

One more massive search of sea and sky around Bermuda was begun. The search continued for more than a week. But no trace of the missing airliner was found. *Star Ariel*, like *Star Tiger*, had vanished from the face of the earth.

Because two airliners of the same type were lost within a relatively short period of time, people wondered whether the fault was in the planes themselves. Could both airliners have been seriously defective in some way?

That doesn't seem to be the case, however. Investigators could find no evidence of serious defects in either plane. Nor could they find major faults in that type of aircraft.

Star Tiger and *Star Ariel* were Tudor IV aircraft manufactured by the British firm of A. V. Roe & Co., Ltd. At the time of the loss of *Star Ariel,* Tudor IV aircraft had been in use for about four years. They were flown on the Berlin Airlift and on air routes around the world. Yet, the only major mishaps with aircraft of that type were the losses of the two airliners near Bermuda.

But those losses were enough to give the planes a bad name. Following the disappearance of *Star Ariel,* Tudor IV airliners were never again used to carry passengers.

The mysterious losses of *Star Tiger* and *Star Ariel* also tended to give the region around Bermuda a bad name. "A jinx," some people whispered, and they wondered "who will be next?"

As far as airplanes were concerned, there was no next for several years. The jinx seemed to be over—until October 30, 1954.

Late in the evening of that day, forty-two passengers climbed aboard a U.S. Navy super-constellation transport plane at Patuxent River Naval Air Station, Maryland. The passengers were bound for the Azores. Actually, they had been part way there, but the plane they were on developed engine trouble. They returned to Patuxent River, and changed planes to the super-constellation.

About an hour and a half after takeoff, the pilot placed the position of the super-constellation north of Bermuda. It was a routine report. And it was the last report from that plane.

When the pilot of the super-constellation failed to make two scheduled position reports, an alarm was given. Search planes winged out over the darkening sea.

At first, the searchers were hampered by darkness. Later, they were hampered by foul weather. No trace of the super-constellation was found, and no cause could be given for the loss.

There was another long pause—then another mysterious plane loss.

On January 8, 1962, a KB-50 refueling tanker aircraft left Langley Air Force Base, Virginia, at 11:17 A.M. The plane was bound for the Azores.

At 1:00 P.M., the pilot of the KB-50 reported the plane's position as 250 miles east of Cape Charles, Virginia. They were on course, on time, and the weather was good. But they failed to report ever again.

Long before the KB-50 was due to land in the Azores, Air Force officials realized that something was wrong. A search was begun.

For more than a week, planes and ships crisscrossed the area. An oil slick was spotted about 300 miles east of Norfolk, Virginia. Did it mark the grave of the KB-50? No one could say for sure. Oil slicks are not uncommon on the sea surface within a few hundred miles of land. No wreckage was ever found. The loss of the KB-50 was another total mystery.

A year and a half later, two more aerial refueling tankers were added to the list of the lost planes. In this case, the tankers were KC-135s—bigger, faster, more modern planes than the KB-50.

On the morning of August 28, 1963, two KC-135 tanker aircraft roared down the runway of Homestead Air Force Base, Florida. Five men were on one plane. Six were on the other. Their mission? Refuel B-47 bombers at a secret rendezvous out over the Atlantic, and then return to Homestead by a roundabout route.

The tankers met the bombers and gave them fuel. Then the tankers continued on an easterly heading. Around noon, the two planes reported their position as 900 miles northeast of Miami and about 260 miles southwest of Bermuda. All was well at that time.

No further reports came in from the two KC-135 tankers. When the planes failed to return to Homestead at the scheduled time, 3:00 P.M., a big search effort was launched.

Unlike the results of searches of other disappearances, these searchers soon found wreckage. In fact, so much wreckage was found that it confused Air Force investigators trying to find a cause for the twin loss. If all the wreckage were found in one place, that would indicate that the planes might have collided in midair. But wreckage sightings were reported from three different areas.

Two large patches of debris were found within a 50-mile area about 300 miles southwest of Bermuda. Some of this debris was identified as coming from one or both KC-135s. Though the two areas of wreckage were found somewhat far apart, their discovery did not rule out the midair collision theory. A collision high in the sky could have showered small chunks of wreckage over a very wide area. If the planes collided, spun apart, and then exploded, that would account for two patches of wreckage relatively far apart.

But what would account for a third patch of wreckage? Debris was spotted about 160 miles away from the major patches of wreckage. That seemed to be the end of the midair collision theory, until a closer look revealed that the debris was seaweed, driftwood, and an old buoy. Therefore, the midair collision theory remains. Investigators concluded that it was likely that the two KC-135s collided about 300 miles southwest of Bermuda. Of course, that was never proved. Many doubts linger on in the minds of people who read and write about air and sea mysteries.

Almost two years later, Homestead Air Force Base was again the stage for a baffling air mystery. On the evening of June 5, 1965, a C-119 flying boxcar transport plane flew eastward from Homestead. The plane was carrying a load of equipment to a U.S. Air Force installation on Grand Turk Island in the Bahamas.

The flight was uneventful. Forty-five minutes before they were due to land at Grand Turk, the pilot of the flying box-car reported the plane's position. And that was it. No other word was heard.

Again there was a search. Again an inquiry. But no clues or cause for the disappearance were found.

East of Florida, south of Bermuda—the plane losses go on. January 1967 brought three in a row.

On January 11, 1967, a twin-engined plane disappeared while it was being used to make a movie near the Bahamas. No warning was given. No distress call was heard. The plane simply flew out from Florida and didn't come back.

Later, some wreckage was found floating about thirty miles northwest of the Bahamas island of Bimini. Investigators figured that the floating wreckage marked the spot where the plane crashed. But no cause for the crash could be found.

Six days later, another plane disappeared. Four people left Miami Airport aboard a Beechcraft Bonanza for a pleasure flight around the Florida Keys. On that day, a plane landed at Key Largo. Four people from the plane had lunch there, then they took off again. A man recalled that the plane's engine sputtered as it climbed skyward. Was that the missing Beechcraft Bonanza? No one can be sure! But one thing is sure—no one saw the Beechcraft Bonanza and its passengers after that.

On January 20, 1967, the third plane was lost on a short flight from San Juan, Puerto Rico to St. Thomas, Virgin Islands. The plane was a single-engined Piper Apache, and it carried the daughter of a U.S. ambassador and her husband. As a result, the search effort was great—but late. The pilot of the plane had failed to file a flight plan. And the plane wasn't missed for almost nine hours after it should have landed at St. Thomas. Thus, the search effort was begun long after the plane was overdue. No trace of the Piper Apache was ever found.

Another Piper aircraft was lost in the region on November 23, 1970. In this case the plane was a Piper Comanche. With a pilot and two passengers aboard, it left West Palm Beach, Florida, at 3:45 in the afternoon. It was bound for Jamaica. Thirty minutes after takeoff, the pilot reported his position. That was the last word heard from the plane. Darkness was closing over the area when a search was begun. No trace of the Piper Comanche was found. It was one more mysterious loss in an area marked by mysterious losses.

Chapter 3
MANY SAILING SHIPS ARE LOST

East of Florida, south of Bermuda. So many planes vanished in that ocean region that the losses have created an atmosphere of mystery and fear about the place—fear that might never be produced by ship losses alone.

Yet, ships were lost there too. As a matter of fact, ship and boat losses greatly outnumber plane losses in the area.

Wasp, *Grampus*, *Atalanta*, *Cyclops*, *Marine Sulphur Queen*, *Anita*—the list is long. Those ships and many, many others sailed into the western Atlantic region, and didn't sail out again.

In the days of sail, such total disappearances were not uncommon. Many a ship left port and was never heard from again. A storm, a sudden gale, uncharted rocks, shifting sands, fire at sea, or pirates might put an end to its voyage.

Therefore, when sailing ships vanished—even big ones like the USS *Wasp* in 1814 and USS *Grampus* in 1843—there seldom was a search or an inquiry. A major exception to this practice was the massive search for HMS *Atalanta* in 1880. But the *Atalanta* loss was a special case.

HMS *Atalanta* was a training ship!

About 200 boys in training to command the ships of Britain's Royal Navy someday were crowded aboard the old

Atalanta. They were there to learn the ways of the sea and ships.

Since the admirals of the Royal Navy believed that future officers could learn good seamanship only aboard a full-rigged sailing ship, the *Atalanta* was a relic from another age. The ship was very much out-of-date by 1880. It was a wooden ship propelled only by the wind at a time when iron ships driven by steam engines were filling the ranks of the world's navies.

Yet, the old *Atalanta* was safe and seaworthy—or at least the admirals thought so. However, this feeling of confidence in the old ship wasn't shared by all the relatives of the boys aboard. Many of those relatives were worried by the memory of a recent tragedy.

In 1878, HMS *Eurydice*, a wooden training ship similar to *Atalanta*, turned turtle (turned upside down) and sank within sight of land. The ship took 300 men and boys to watery graves.

The loss of the *Eurydice* created the need for another large training ship of wood and canvas.

HMS *Atalanta* was the last of a line of wooden warships that had served Britain well for hundreds of years. Under the name HMS *Juno,* the ship entered the Royal Navy as a 64-gun frigate in 1845. It was a fine warship. But it was soon hopelessly out of date. The development of steam engines, armor plating, and rifled cannon made HMS *Juno* obsolete. The ship's name was changed from *Juno* to *Atalanta.* In 1865, the out-of-date warship was retired to serve as a police hulk in Portsmouth harbor. That's how the *Atalanta* might have ended its days—except for the loss of the *Eurydice.*

With the *Eurydice* gone, the Royal Navy needed another ship of "the old school" to take classes of midshipmen on long training voyages. *Atalanta* met the need. In 1879, the old ship was towed out of Portsmouth harbor, dusted off, cleaned up, and refitted as a training ship.

As a training ship, HMS *Atalanta* would carry no guns. As

a result, the ship tended to be top heavy. The masts were too tall, and the spars were too wide for a gunless ship.

Capt. Francis Stirling, the man appointed to command the training ship, suggested that the masts be shortened, the rigging be lightened, and the ballast increased.

No one knows how many of these changes were made by the time HMS *Atalanta* set sail from Portsmouth on November 7, 1879. Whether or not all the changes were made on time was to be a subject for argument over the years to come.

In November 1879, HMS *Atalanta* sailed southwestward from England toward the West Indies. The ship passed by the Azores, stopped briefly at Barbados, and sailed on to Bermuda.

Storms and sickness troubled the voyage. When HMS *Atalanta* sailed into Hamilton Harbor, Bermuda, on January 29, 1880, ship and crew were fairly battered.

At that point, Capt. Stirling evidently decided to shorten the voyage of the *Atalanta.* The training ship had been scheduled to sail north to Nova Scotia and then down into the Caribbean Sea before returning to England. In a letter to his wife, sent on January 30, Capt. Stirling said that the *Atalanta* would sail directly from Bermuda to England. He expected the ship to reach England during the first week in March 1880.

On January 31, 1880, the *Atalanta* sailed out of Hamilton Harbor, bound for England. The ship was never seen again.

When the *Atalanta* didn't reach England during the first week in March, there was no alarm. Only Capt. Stirling's wife expected the ship to return at that time, and she knew enough about the ways of the sea and of seamen to expect long delays. Officers of the Royal Navy and relatives of the *Atalanta* midshipmen didn't expect the ship to return until the first week in April. That was the originally scheduled return date. The officers and relatives didn't know of Capt. Stirling's change in plans.

The first week in April passed without a sign of HMS

Atalanta. Some relatives were already worried. By the end of the second week, telegrams and letters started to pour into the Admiralty, the head office of the Royal Navy.

Then a newspaper disclosed that the *Atalanta* had sailed from Bermuda for England on January 31, and thus the ship was more than a month overdue. This information triggered a march of relatives on the Admiralty. "Where is the *Atalanta*?" was the cry.

Admiralty officials replied that the *Atalanta* had probably been delayed by a storm. That was not unusual in the days of sail. "*Atalanta* will show up," Admiralty officials assured the concerned relatives. "Just wait and see."

But the relatives wouldn't wait. So on April 18, 1880, the Admiralty sent the stores ship HMS *Wye* as far as the Azores to look for the *Atalanta.* The crew of the stores ship found no trace of the overdue training ship. The captain of the *Wye* said that he doubted that the *Atalanta* had ever reached the Azores.

By the first of May, British newspapers were severely criticizing the Royal Navy. They compared the disappearance of the *Atalanta* to the loss of the *Eurydice.* "Why should innocent boys be sent to sea in unsafe ships?" the papers asked.

Admiralty officials replied that the *Atalanta* was "a very safe vessel."

But the *Atalanta* was missing!

All the criticism of their training program and ship selection upset officials of the Royal Navy. As a result, they did something on May 5, 1880, that they'd never done before. They launched a massive search for an overdue ship. Five fast warships were sent to "comb the sea from Bantry Bay (Ireland) to the Azores . . . and back again" for some sign of the *Atalanta.*

Though such a search had never been made before, relatives of the *Atalanta* midshipmen felt that it was not enough. They believed that the search should go all the way to Bermuda.

But the search vessels didn't go that far. They "combed the sea" between England and the Azores. They found no trace of *Atalanta* or of the 290 men who were on the training ship.

On May 12, the Royal Navy called off the search and opened an inquiry.

What happened to the *Atalanta*? When was the ship lost? Where was it lost?

No one knows!

The inquiry provided no real answers. Some witnesses said that the *Atalanta* was a "cranky ship" that could easily turn turtle. Other witnesses said that it was an extremely stable ship that could turn over only in the worst of storms.

During the summer months of 1880, many "messages" from the lost *Atalanta* were reported. But these messages turned out to be fakes.

The *Atalanta* could have sunk any time between January 31 and early March in 1880. A storm raged in the mid-Atlantic during early February. But it's unlikely that the slow-sailing *Atalanta* would have reached that area of ocean during the first or second week of February. Another storm raged around the Azores in early April. But it now seems likely that the *Atalanta* was lost before that time.

February and March are very stormy months in the North Atlantic. The *Atalanta* could have run into a storm not reported by any other ship.

That brings up the question of where the ship was lost. The *Atalanta* could have been lost anywhere along the route from Bermuda to England. However, many ships—refugees from the mid-Atlantic storm—were heading westward toward Bermuda in early February 1880. And none of those ships reported sighting the *Atalanta*. What's more, no ship on the well-traveled route from Bermuda to England sighted the *Atalanta*.

If the *Atalanta* had progressed far along its course to

England, the training ship would surely have crossed paths with ships sailing westward from Europe. That's not all. The old slow *Atalanta* would surely have been overtaken by several fast steamships traveling along the same route toward Europe.

But from the moment the *Atalanta* left Hamilton Harbor, the training ship was never seen again. It would seem likely that the *Atalanta* was lost in the western Atlantic fairly close to Bermuda.

Chapter 4
STEAMSHIPS TOO!

In the years following the loss of the *Atalanta,* many other ships and boats vanished in the western Atlantic region around Bermuda. But there was no other single great loss of lives in the area until March 1918.

On March 4, 1918, the United States Ship *Cyclops* sailed northwestward from Barbados on the final leg of a voyage from Rio de Janeiro, Brazil to Baltimore, Maryland. The USS *Cyclops* left Barbados and was never seen again. Three hundred and nine people—73 passengers and 236 crewmen—vanished with the ship.

At the time, the disappearance of the *Cyclops* was not considered a great mystery. Why not? In March 1918, the United States and Germany were at war. It was assumed that the USS *Cyclops* had been torpedoed and sunk by a German submarine.

It wasn't until December 1918—a month after the war had ended—that U.S. naval officers learned that there had been no German submarines in the western Atlantic during March 1918. That discovery brought up the question: What could have happened to the USS *Cyclops*?

The USS *Cyclops* was a collier, a coal-carrying ship. But when the *Cyclops* sailed from Brazil bound for Baltimore in 1918, the ship wasn't carrying coal. It was loaded with 10,800 tons of manganese ore.

Could that cargo have been directly responsible for the loss of the *Cyclops*?

This question occurred to U.S. navy officers when acts of war, mutiny, and piracy were ruled out as possible causes of the ship's loss. A few officers concluded that the cargo of ore could indeed have been the cause of *Cyclops'* disappearance.

One officer suggested that the manganese ore might have suddenly shifted to one side in the ship's hold. Such a shift of the load could have caused the ship to roll over.

Another officer claimed that the ore was badly loaded in the ship—too much weight at either end and not enough in the middle. In that officers' opinion, the strain set up by the unbalanced load was enough to crack the ship in two.

Most naval safety experts don't agree with these notions. They say that ore is unlikely to shift around in a ship's hold. They also say that a loaded ship is unlikely to turn over except in extremely stormy weather.

U.S.S. *Cyclops* left Barbados on March 4, 1918, bound for Baltimore and was never seen again. (*N.Y. Public Library*)

In answer to the suggestion that *Cyclops* broke in two, the experts point out that there's no evidence that the ship was badly loaded. But even if it were badly loaded, the ship would be very unlikely to break up, except in extremely stormy weather.

Did *Cyclops* encounter extremely stormy weather?

No major storms were reported from the area through which *Cyclops* was scheduled to sail in March 1918. When *Cyclops* left Barbados, the sky was clear and the sea was calm.

War, weather, or dangerous cargo cannot explain the total disappearance of the USS *Cyclops* and the 309 people on the ship. That disappearance continues to be one of the great unsolved mysteries of the sea.

Dangerous cargo might, however, explain another ship loss in the western Atlantic. On February 2, 1963, the S.S. *Marine Sulphur Queen* left Beaumont, Texas. It was bound for Norfolk, Virginia, with a cargo of molten sulphur. The *Marine Sulphur Queen* was in radio contact with several stations until the morning of February 4, when the ship rounded the Florida Keys and passed into the Atlantic. Then there was silence. The S.S. *Marine Sulphur Queen* had vanished!

However, the disappearance was not complete. Life jackets, oil cans, a broken oar, a man's shirt, and chunks of wood were found in the water near the Florida Keys. Some of this debris was identified as coming from the *Marine Sulphur Queen.* All the signs pointed to a sudden unexpected disaster overtaking the sulphur-carrying ship as it sailed from the Gulf of Mexico into the Atlantic Ocean.

But what was the nature of the disaster?

That was the question a U.S. Coast Guard board of inquiry had to answer. After sifting through all available evidence, the board of inquiry gave not one but five answers.

Board members suggested that an explosion could have

occurred in the ship's cargo area. Though molten sulphur has been carried safely by other ships, it is a dangerous substance. When hot liquid sulphur sloshes around, gases and vapors pour out of the substance. It is known that the *Marine Sulphur Queen* encountered rough seas on the way out of the Gulf of Mexico. Therefore, the ship's liquid cargo must have been sloshed around a lot. That means that gases and vapors in the cargo area could have built up to an explosive level. If those gases exploded, they would have ripped the ship apart without warning.

However, the wreckage recovered from the water showed no signs that such an explosion took place within the cargo tank. An explosion of the sulphurous gases in the tank would surely have left flash marks and tiny traces of sulphur on most of the ship. Yet none of the recovered debris was charred, and no trace of sulphur was found on any of it.

The board of inquiry offered another possibility. Perhaps the hull of the *Marine Sulphur Queen* had been ruptured by an explosion of steam. Such a steam explosion would not be likely to leave flash marks or signs of sulphur on the ship's wreckage. But what could have produced enough steam under pressure to blast a hole in the ship?

Coast Guard investigators explained that if sea water seeped into the vicinity of the cargo tank, steam would form as the cold water touched the hot tank of molten sulphur.

Sea water could have seeped into the cargo area when the ship traveled through rough seas. As a result, sufficient steam pressure might have built up to blast a hole in the ship's hull.

But there are a few things wrong with the theory. If sea water were seeping into the cargo area, crew members would surely have spotted the danger. It's also likely that the ship's pumps would have automatically discharged large amounts of sea water. Furthermore, the build-up of steam near the cargo tank would have produced various symptoms of trouble before the point of explosion. But no hint of trouble was given in the ship's radio messages. No distress signal was sent by the *Marine Sulphur Queen.*

Did the *Marine Sulphur Queen* capsize unexpectedly?

"It is quite possible that the ship rolled over and sank without warning," the board of inquiry stated. Reports that the *Marine Sulphur Queen* had been rolling rapidly were received from the ship on the day before all contact was lost. Though the rolling motion was considered not dangerous at the time, the motion could have increased. The ship's liquid cargo could have added to the problem. The more the ship rolled, the more the liquid cargo would have sloshed from side to side, adding to the rolling motion.

However, board of inquiry members noted there was no report that the ship's speed had been slowed. The captain would surely have ordered a decrease in speed if the rolling motion were severe.

The board of inquiry also raised the possibility that the *Marine Sulphur Queen* may have broken in two. In 1960, the ship was converted from an oil tanker into a sulphur carrier. That changeover involved removing all the transverse bulkheads in the ship. Transverse bulkheads are the internal walls that separate the ship's hull into watertight compartments. These bulkheads also reinforce the hull. Their removal might have seriously weakened the *Marine Sulphur Queen's* structure. Then the action of the stormy waves and the motion of the ship's cargo could have produced enough strain to crack the ship's hull. Without watertight compartments to limit flooding, the ship would rapidly fill with water and sink.

That's not all. A ship's structural strength is related to its age. The older a ship gets, the weaker it becomes. In 1963, the S.S. *Marine Sulphur Queen* was almost twenty years old —a dangerous age for a tanker.

The age of the ship, its weakened structure, the nature of its cargo, and the type of sea it was sailing through support the conclusion that the *Marine Sulphur Queen* broke in two. However, the absence of a sulphur slick on the sea surface where the ship's debris was found works against this conclusion. If the ship had split in two, it is most likely that all of its cargo would have been spilled into the sea. But the search planes could spot no sign of the sulphur.

Still another possible explanation for the loss of the *Marine Sulphur Queen* was offered by the Coast Guard commandant. He noted that in sulphur-carrying ships, certain gases tended to accumulate in the areas around the cargo tanks. A build-up of such gases in the *Marine Sulphur Queen* could have resulted in an explosion that could have ruptured the ship's hull. In that case, the ship would have sunk with the cargo tank intact. No sulphur or sulphurous gases would have been released.

Though such a gas build-up and explosion seems unlikely, it is not beyond the realm of possibility.

The disappearance of the *Marine Sulphur Queen* is still unsolved. By providing a grab bag of possible causes for the loss of the ship, the Coast Guard left an aura of mystery hanging over the disappearance of the ship.

The disappearance of the Norwegian ship *Anita* in 1973 provides an interesting contrast to the loss of the *Marine Sulphur Queen.* The *Anita* sailed out of Norfolk, Virginia, bound for Germany. Two days after leaving port, the *Anita* vanished. No distress call was received from the ship. Unlike the *Marine Sulphur Queen,* the *Anita* did not leave a pile of debris and a long list of possible causes for its loss behind.

However, also unlike the loss of the *Marine Sulphur Queen,* the loss of the *Anita* is not considered a great unsolved mystery. Why not?

The loss of another Norwegian ship, the *Norse Variant,* gave investigators a strong clue as to what happened to *Anita.*

Two hours before *Anita*, the *Norse Variant* sailed out of Norfolk, Virginia, on March 21, 1973. Two days later, the *Norse Variant's* radio operator reported that the ship had run into a fierce storm in the Atlantic, and as a result it was foundering. The last call from the *Norse Variant* stated that the crew were taking to the boats.

Rescue ships and planes headed out to sea to pick up the survivors. Three days later, one survivor was found. He described how the *Norse Variant* was ripped apart and flooded by raging winds and towering seas.

Since the *Anita* was traveling along the same course right behind the *Norse Variant*, it is assumed that *Anita* sailed into the same fierce storm. Although no SOS was received from *Anita* and no survivors were found, it is also assumed that *Anita* suffered the same fate as the *Norse Variant*.

East of Florida, south of Bermuda—ships and planes continue to vanish in that ocean region. Reasonable explanations can be found for some of the losses. Many other losses baffle the experts. With each baffling loss, the legend of fear and mystery about that ocean region has grown. People have asked, "Who or what is stealing all those ships and planes?"

Chapter 5

AND A TERRIBLE TRIANGLE IS BORN —IN PRINT

• On a clear day, a seaworthy ship with a brave crew sails out of port and is never seen again. Inbound ships that should have crossed its path can report no sign of the missing vessel. There's no wreckage. There are no survivors. What strange fate claimed that ship? What ocean limbo holds it?

• Sails set, a crewless ship glides like a ghost out of the sea fog. All is ship-shape on its decks. There are no signs of struggle or of storm damage. Personal belongings are all there. But where have all the crewmen gone?

• Without a puff of wind to fill its sails, a ship lies still in a glass-smooth sea. Weeds float on the still water. Small creatures hop among the weeds. Here and there, chunks of wreckage appear trapped among the seaweed. What strange sea is this? Can it be a graveyard of lost ships?

• Clouds hide the moon. The night sky is dark. Yet the sea glows! What magic source of light is that? What monsters lurk beneath the waves to threaten poor sailors?

Ever since people first went down to the sea in ships, there have been stories of sea monsters. Tales such as these have been told by old sailors and retold inside book covers.

Many a tale has concerned strange happenings and total disappearances of ships and boats in the western region of the Atlantic Ocean. For more than a hundred years, writers have noted the high number of unexplained ship losses in the area between the east coast of the United States and Bermuda. As a result, that ocean area has at various times been called the "Sea of Lost Ships," the "Hoodoo Sea," the "Limbo of the Lost," and the "Sea of Oblivion."

Up to the 1940s, each disappearance of a ship or boat in the area was viewed as a separate mystery of the sea. Though the stormy nature of the particular sea area might be a factor common to many of the losses, writers usually looked for an individual cause for each loss. That cause might be a certain storm, a flaw in the vessel, or human error.

Then in December 1945, the five airplanes of Flight 19 vanished without a trace in the area. That added a new dimension to the mysteries. The "Sea of Lost Ships" had become a "Skytrap" as well.

More ships and more planes disappeared. People began to wonder, "Could forces other than those of nature be responsible for all the strange losses of ships and planes?"

During the early 1950s several newspapers, particularly in Florida, carried articles about the strange disappearances of so many ships and planes in the ocean area near Florida. "Sea Mystery at Our Back Door," one headline announced. All the new mysteries were covered in detail. Most of the old mysteries of the region were searched out and retold. The public was very interested.

At the same time, a UFO (unidentified flying object) flap was on. Reports of "flying saucer" sightings poured in from around the world. Even a few "saucer landings" were reported. Strange creatures were said to visit earth.

Could these flying saucers and unearthly creatures have

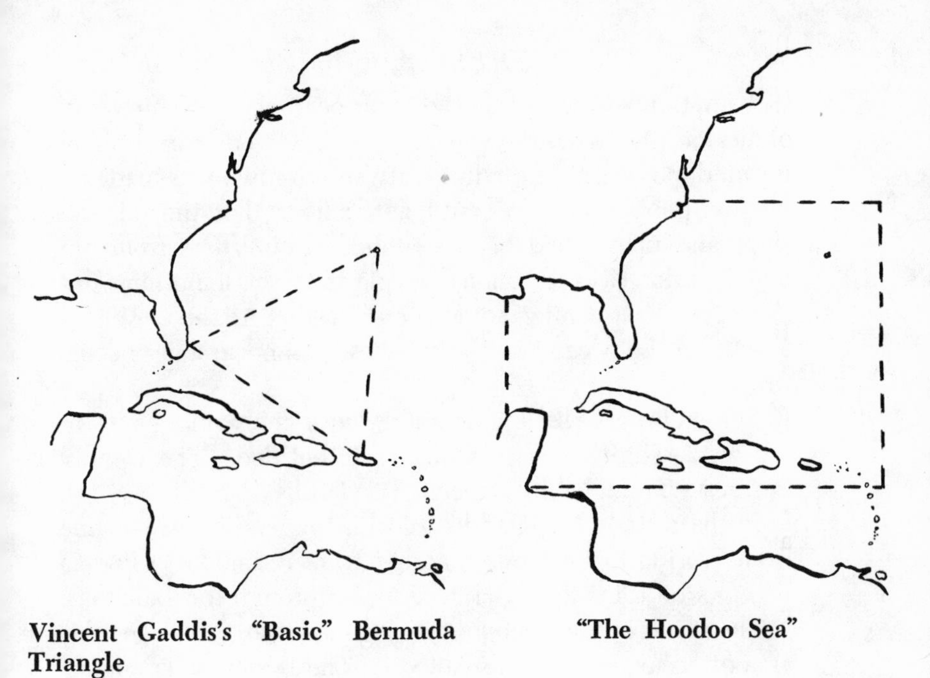

Vincent Gaddis's "Basic" Bermuda Triangle

"The Hoodoo Sea"

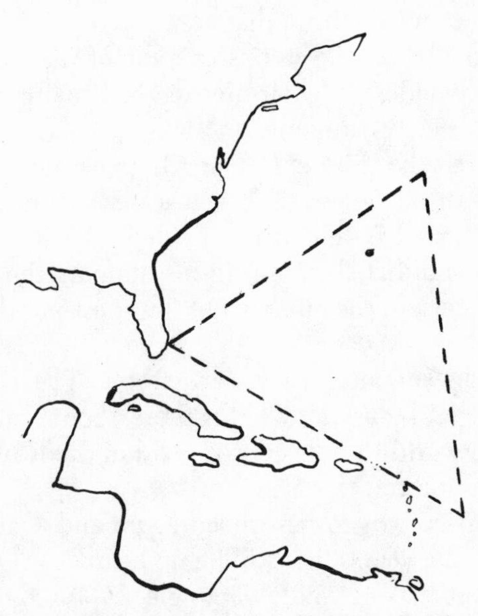

Spencer's "Limbo of the Lost" The Extended Triangle

had anything to do with the disappearances of ships and planes in the Atlantic Ocean area between Florida and Bermuda? Naturally, the link between the two was made.

Most people, however, did not believe that the missing ships and planes had been snatched by invaders from another world. Even so, many people felt that something unusual was happening somewhere in the Atlantic. Where exactly in the ocean were all of these disappearances occurring?

The February 1964 issue of *Argosy* magazine gave an "answer." The answer was an article entitled, "The Deadly Bermuda Triangle" by Vincent H. Gaddis.

In that article Mr. Gaddis told his readers to draw a line from Florida to Bermuda, another from Bermuda to Puerto Rico, and a third line back to Florida through the Bahamas.

The result of all this line drawing on a map is a triangular area of ocean. Mr. Gaddis called it "The Bermuda Triangle." He claimed that most of the total vanishments of ships and planes occurred within that area.

Mr. Gaddis retold the stories of some of the "total vanishments." He wondered "what menace lurks within a triangle of tragedy so close to home."

But couldn't the ship and plane disappearances have been caused by natural events, and their losses within a particular area be explained by chance coincidence?

Mr. Gaddis didn't think so. In his opinion, the number of disappearances in the area went far beyond the laws of chance.

Mr. Gaddis summed up his article on "The Deadly Bermuda Triangle" by asking what is there about that particular piece of the world that has destroyed hundreds of ships and planes without a trace?

That question was to be echoed again and again by other writers over the years. It is still being heard.

The idea of a Bermuda Triangle captured the public

imagination. Here was an easily identified area of ocean into which ships and planes traveled—and vanished never to be seen again.

Writers tended to no longer look for the causes of ship and plane disappearances in the events that happened aboard those ships and planes. Instead they looked for answers to the riddle of the losses in the nature of the relatively small chunk of ocean known as the "Bermuda Triangle."

By "creating" the Bermuda Triangle, Vincent Gaddis put a boundary around many sea mysteries and made them one. That set the stage for extraterrestrial (beyond earth), supernatural (beyond nature), and lost civilization "explanations" for ship and plane disappearances within the "deadly triangle."

According to one of these "explanations," the ship and plane losses were accidently caused by the work of invaders from another world. The invaders come to earth in flying

Old sailors believed that sea monsters attacked ships in the ocean area around Bermuda. This sea monster was said to have been seen near Bermuda by the crew of the ship, *British Banner*.

saucers. They have a base at the bottom of the sea near the center of the area known as the Bermuda Triangle. This base in the sea has a huge power plant. When that power plant is working, it sucks down everything that's on the sea, in the sea, and even far above the sea.

A variation of that "flying saucer" theme disagrees that the losses of ships and planes were accidental. By this account, certain ships and planes are selected for close examination by the unearthly invaders. When a ship or plane is selected, it is wrapped in "an electromagnetic net." That "net" blocks all radio signals to or from the vehicle. Thus shut off from the outside world, the trapped vehicle is lowered down, down to the invaders' base beneath the waves.

The idea that the Bermuda Triangle is caused not by present-day unearthly invaders, but by the leftover technology of a bygone earthly civilization has been advanced by a few writers. They say that it's possible that the lost continent of Atlantis lies directly beneath the ocean area called the Bermuda Triangle. In that case, a giant destructive machine left there by a vanished civilization could from time to time send out deadly rays that would vaporize any passing ship or plane. The writers figure that the destructive machine might be triggered to send out those deadly rays by certain positions of the moon and stars in the sky.

It was also suggested that the missing ships and planes might be trapped in a "time tunnel." That, according to some people, is a place beyond time where objects are held in an "invisible dimension."

Most scientists consider that "explanation" to be a lot of meaningless gobbledegook. However, it is fairly widely accepted by readers of Bermuda Triangle books.

The late Ivan Sanderson, founder of the Society for the Investigation of the Unexplained, said that the Bermuda Triangle was but one of twelve places on the earth's surface where "strange things happen." He suggested that "something is wrong with time" in those places. Some other people have suggested that the twelve places are the sites of gravitational and magnetic whirlpools. But they didn't clearly explain what that meant.

These "explanations" for the mysterious losses of ships and planes in the western Atlantic are far from dull. But there isn't a shred of evidence to support any of them. They're based on the assumption that most or all of the mysterious disappearances occurred within a relatively small, easily defined area of ocean, known as the Bermuda Triangle. Therefore, some strange power must exist in that ocean area.

However, did most of the disappearances of ships and planes occur in the area defined by Vincent Gaddis as the Bermuda Triangle?

Chapter 6
BUT WHY A TRIANGLE?

There is a place—a triangular section of the Atlantic Ocean —that swallows ships and planes. It is called the Bermuda Triangle.

Vincent Gaddis gave this concept to the world, and much of the world became interested and intrigued by the notion of a mysterious ship-swallowing slice of sea. Many separate sea and air mysteries were bundled together to form one great mystery—the mystery of the deadly Bermuda Triangle.

"What strange forces lie hidden in that triangle of seemingly peaceful sea?" became a frequent question. Writers, explorers, investigators of the unknown, weathermen, sailors, and skin divers tried to give an answer.

More than a dozen books and close to a hundred magazine and newspaper articles have been written about the Bermuda Triangle, also known as the Devil's Triangle. Many talks and lectures have been given on the subject, and at least one movie and one television program have been made about the mysterious "Triangle of Terror."

Thanks to all this attention, the many mysteries that make up the story of the Bermuda Triangle have been listed, sifted, mapped, researched, debated, and analyzed. As a result, one thing has become quite clear: the Bermuda Triangle that was first mapped out by Vincent Gaddis isn't big enough to cover all the puzzling disappearances of ships and planes in the western Atlantic. What's more, the shape is wrong.

Vincent Gaddis marked off the Bermuda Triangle with imaginary lines from Miami, Florida, to Bermuda; from Bermuda to Puerto Rico; and from Puerto Rico to Miami. These imaginary boundaries have made it easy to locate the Triangle on a map. However, many of the unexplained ship and plane disappearances in the western Atlantic seem to have occurred outside that area. In other words, many, if not most, of the Bermuda Triangle mysteries are located outside the Bermuda Triangle!

HMS *Atalanta* surely disappeared outside that triangular slice of sea. The ship vanished while enroute from Bermuda to England. The airliner *Star Tiger* never reached the area. The plane disappeared somewhere between the Azores and Bermuda.

It now seems certain that the *Marine Sulphur Queen* never entered the Bermuda Triangle. Neither did the *Anita* and the *Norse Variant.*

The super constellation aircraft that disappeared while enroute from Patuxent River, Maryland, to the Azores should have passed well to the north of the Bermuda Triangle. The same thing can be said for the KB-50 aerial tanker that vanished between Langley Air Force Base, Virginia, and the Azores.

Many of the other ships and planes that were said to have disappeared within the Bermuda Triangle were on courses that would not have taken them into the Triangle. Some of the planes and ships that were on course for the Bermuda Triangle were reported missing before they reached the area. Others are known to have safely sailed through the Triangle before they vanished.

Very few of the "Bermuda Triangle disappearances" can be said with certainty to have occurred within the Bermuda

Triangle as it was originally mapped out by Vincent Gaddis.

This uncertainty posed great difficulties for the many writers who rushed to explore the fascinating mystery of the Bermuda Triangle.

Most of the writers, however, tried to get out of the difficulty by enlarging the Triangle or by changing its shape to include most of the air and sea mysteries of the western Atlantic region.

Sports writer Aubrey Graves of *The Washington Post* gave the "Triangle" a fan shape. He anchored the base of the "fan" on Bermuda, and he stretched one end as far north as Long Island, New York, and the other end went down to the Virgin Islands.

Leslie Lieber gave the mysterious ocean area a square shape straddling Bermuda. Ivan Sanderson said that the area of the mysterious disappearances was lozenge-shaped. In his opinion it was but one of several lozenge-shaped danger areas located around the world.

In his book, *The Devil's Triangle,* Richard Winer contends that the "Triangle" is not a triangle at all. He says, "It is a trapezium, a four-sided area in which no two sides or angles are the same. And the first four letters of the word *trapezium* more than adequately describes it."

Adi-Kent Thomas Jeffrey shows two sides of the "Triangle" in his book, *The Bermuda Triangle*—one running from Norfolk, Virginia, to Bermuda, and the other from Bermuda to Puerto Rico. He leaves the third side open. He describes the Bermuda Triangle as " . . . a mystery zone where thousands of men and hundreds of ships and planes have been disappearing for years without a trace and utterly without any explanation."

Another book entitled *The Bermuda Triangle* makes a similar claim. This particular book has been a "best seller." It is written by Charles Berlitz, a noted skin diver, explorer, and author. Mr. Berlitz considers the Bermuda Triangle to

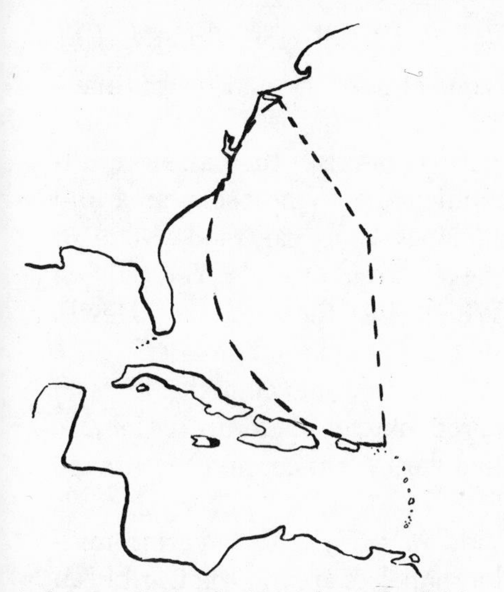

Aubrey Graves' Fan-shaped "Triangle"

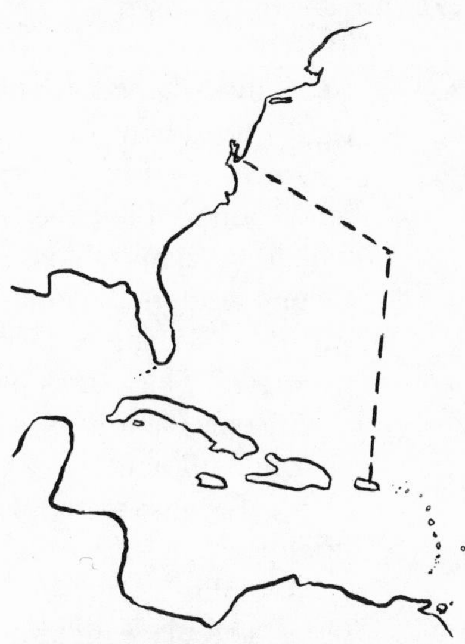

Richard Winer's "Trapezium"

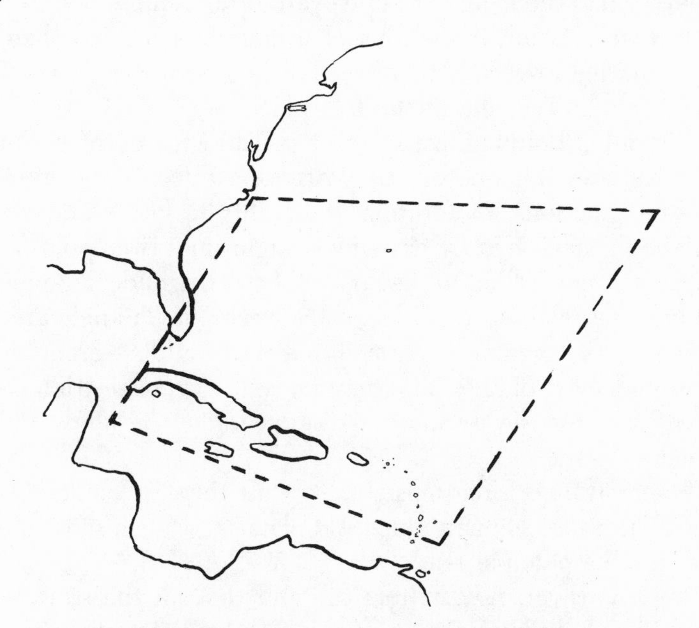

Adi-Kent Thomas Jeffrey's Open-sided "Triangle"

be an oval-shaped oceanic zone of mystery that doesn't have rigidly fixed boundaries.

Graves, Lieber, Winer, Jeffrey, Berlitz—they all have different ideas about the size and shape of the ocean area into which so many ships and planes have vanished. None of them considers the area to be an actual triangle. Yet, they all call it a "Triangle." Mr. Winer calls the area the "Devil's Triangle." The others call it the "Bermuda Triangle."

Vincent Gaddis is sorry now that he coined the term "Bermuda Triangle." He regrets having made up the phrase " . . . because it implies boundaries that contain the strange disappearances."

"Actually," Mr. Gaddis said in 1975, "these marine mysteries take place all around a shapeless area in the Caribbean Sea and on out into the Atlantic Ocean, including part of the Sargasso Sea, the legendary graveyard of lost ships."

However, wasn't it the idea of a boundary around these many marine mysteries that created the one big mystery of the Bermuda Triangle in the first place?

Without a doubt, the notion of a distinct area of ocean that swallows ships and planes without a trace excited people's imaginations. In addition, the ability to locate and define the mystery area by drawing straight lines from point to point on a map added to the appeal of the Bermuda Triangle notion. The relative smallness of the Bermuda Triangle area —as it was originally mapped out by Gaddis—probably prompted most of the "supernatural and extraterrestrial explanations" for the mysterious disappearances of ships and planes.

"Some strange force must be at work there," people reasoned, "to cause so many ships and planes to vanish suddenly in so small a patch of sea."

Now, however, few writers contend that all the strange, unexplained disappearances of ships and planes took place within "so small a patch of sea." Some versions of the Bermuda Triangle mystery include all unexplained disappearances of ships and planes in the western Atlantic Ocean, in the Caribbean Sea, and in the Gulf of Mexico. For instance, the loss of a U.S. Air Force C-124 transport plane on a flight from Newfoundland to Ireland in March, 1951, is often listed as a Bermuda Triangle disappearance. Yet, this plane would have flown far north of anyone's definition of the Bermuda Triangle. The loss of the nuclear submarine USS *Scorpion* is usually included in accounts of the Bermuda Triangle mystery. Yet, wreckage of the *Scorpion* was photographed on the ocean floor 400 miles southwest of the Azores. That's a long, long way from Bermuda. The final resting place of *Scorpion* is much closer to Africa than to America.

South of the Azores, east of Newfoundland, west of Florida —many of the "Bermuda Triangle losses" are widely scattered. This raises some questions. If it had been said origi-

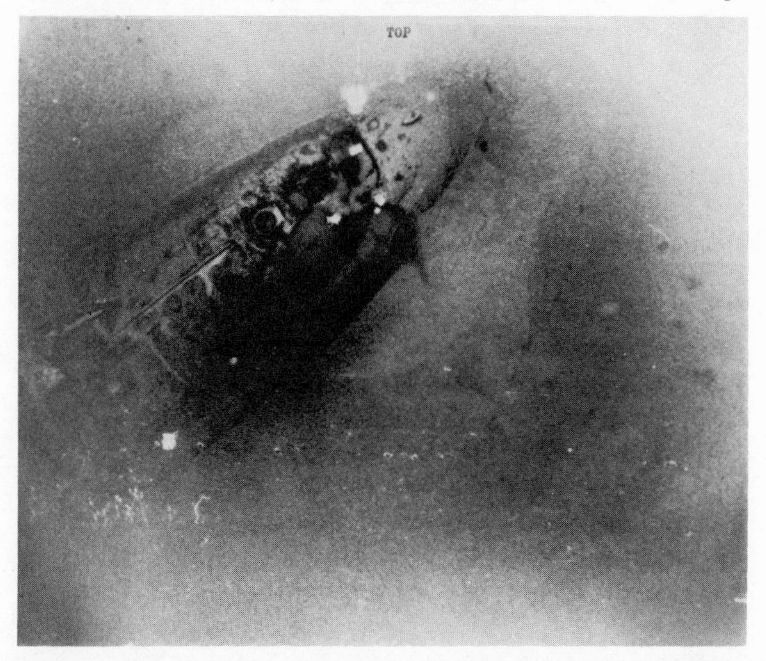

Sunken submarine *Scorpion* at the bottom of the sea. (*Wide World*)

nally that all of the unexplained losses took place around a shapeless area in the Caribbean and far out into the Atlantic Ocean, would the losses have been lumped together into one sea mystery? Or would each loss have been considered as a separate, independent mystery? Would anyone have considered these losses to be part of one mystery if a clearly defined boundary had not been placed around all or most of the strange disappearances of ships and planes in the Atlantic Ocean? Since this boundary has been removed, does that mean an end to the big mystery? Is there—or has there ever really been—a Bermuda Triangle mystery?

Chapter 7
MYSTERY SOLVED?

"At last! The Bermuda Triangle Mystery has been solved!"

Big, bold, black letters headlined this claim in the pages of many American newspapers and magazines during the spring of 1975. The claim was part of an advertisement for a most unusual book—*The Bermuda Triangle Mystery—Solved.*

This book by Lawrence David Kusche differs from all other books about the Bermuda Triangle mystery. In this book, the author argues that there is no such mystery!

"The Legend of the Bermuda Triangle is a manufactured mystery." Mr. Kusche writes. He believes that the mystery was first started by careless research into the disappearances of certain ships and planes in the western Atlantic region. Mr. Kusche argues that some details were left out or garbled in various accounts of these disappearances. As time passed, writers tended to "fill in the missing details" with mysterious guesses. Faulty information led to faulty conclusions, and the great "Bermuda Triangle mystery" was "born."

Lawrence Kusche contends that writers of the Bermuda Triangle "legend" seldom checked the "facts" on each mysterious ship and plane disappearance. Instead, they accepted each other's stories of the disappearances as truth. As a result, error was piled on error.

Lawrence Kusche did check the "facts." He discovered that a few of the "Bermuda Triangle disappearances" never occurred. Several others took place far from the "Triangle." Many of the disappearances that did occur within the "Triangle" could, in Mr. Kusche's opinion, be reasonably explained in terms of natural causes and human error.

How did Lawrence Kusche reach these conclusions?

Just as his book is different from other Bermuda Triangle books, Lawrence David Kusche differs from most of the other people who have written about the Bermuda Triangle mystery. Mr. Kusche is not a skin diver or a seafaring explorer. He is not an expert on UFO's. Neither is he an investigator of the occult.

Lawrence David Kusche is a librarian.

Mr. Kusche works at the Hayden Library of the Arizona State University in Tempe, Arizona—far from the Bermuda Triangle. In fact, Mr. Kusche has never been to the Bermuda Triangle.

Library work triggered Mr. Kusche's interest in the Bermuda Triangle. In 1972, many students asked Mr. Kusche for information about the area. At first, Mr. Kusche couldn't find much readily available information. He probed deeper.

The accounts Mr. Kusche found seemed incomplete in many ways. There were gaps, flaws, and hasty conclusions. He probed even deeper.

Case by case, Lawrence Kusche tracked down each available scrap of information on the missing ships and planes of the Bermuda Triangle. He read old newspaper accounts of the disappearances. He talked to marine and aviation experts. He drew on his own experience as a private airplane pilot and flight instructor. He wrote to government agencies, shipping lines, and insurance companies. He studied old weather records. He examined shipping lists and sailing schedules.

All this checking and double-checking turned up several surprises, including the case of "the ship that never was."

A Norwegian ship named the *Stavenger* is said to have disappeared within the Bermuda Triangle in 1931. Vincent Gaddis wrote that forty-three persons vanished with the ship. According to Charles Berlitz, the *Stavenger* was last located near Cat Island in the Bahamas. Then it vanished.

Most books about the Bermuda Triangle mystery mention the loss of the *Stavenger*. But none of the books give details about the ship, its crew, its cargo, or its course. They do not describe the circumstances surrounding the disappearance either.

Lawrence Kusche searched for more information about the loss of the *Stavenger*. Since it was said that the ship disappeared in October 1931, Mr. Kusche checked newspapers of the period. He went through copies of the London *Times,* of the Bahamas paper *The Nassau Guardian,* and of *The New York Times.* This research revealed that two storms raged near Cat Island during October 1931. But Kusche could find no mention of the loss of a ship named *Stavenger.* He wondered whether a ship with forty-three persons aboard could disappear and not be reported in the newspapers. He checked further. He contacted the big insurance company, Lloyds of London. They keep records of all ships lost at sea. But they had no record of the loss of a ship named *Stavenger.* Mr. Kusche looked through the *Dictionary of Disasters at Sea.* It didn't list such a loss.

Finally, Mr. Kusche wrote to the Norwegian Ministry of Shipping to find out if there ever was a Norwegian ship named *Stravenger.* There wasn't! However, there once was a Norwegian ship named S/S *Stavanger.* This ship was launched in 1925, and was totally wrecked in 1957.

Other ships reported lost in the Bermuda Triangle may never have actually existed. Many of the books about the

Bermuda Triangle mystery briefly mention the disappearances of the Swedish ship *Lotta* in 1866, the Spanish ship *Viego* in 1868, and the Italian ship *Miramon* in 1884. However, despite an extensive search, Mr. Kusche could find no information about the three ships. He could find no records of their losses or even of their existence.

In a very different way, Lawrence Kusche was able to trim another ship disappearance from the Bermuda Triangle "tragedy list." Most Bermuda Triangle books say that the German sailing ship *Freya* vanished in 1902 while enroute from Manzanillo, Cuba to Punta Arenas, Chile. Some accounts say that the ship was later found floating deserted and abandoned. But they don't say where the abandoned ship was found.

There are two Manzanillos in the world. They are both seaports. One of these ports is located on the south coast of Cuba, and the other is located on the west coast of Mexico.

Lost lands beneath the sea have generally been part of the Bermuda Triangle legend. Scientists usually scoffed at the lost lands and lost civilization stories. Then in the late 1960s, scientists from the Woods Hole Oceanographic Institution proved that there are lost lands beneath the surface of the Atlantic. The oceanographers found a chain of underwater mountain peaks ranging from New England to Bermuda. At one time, most of those peaks were above the water surface. But it's unlikely that advanced civilizations lived on those islands. The islands were drowned about 40 million years ago. (*Woods Hole Oceanographic Institution*)

From his research, Mr. Kusche learned that the *Freya* sailed out of the Mexican port of Manzanillo. That means that the entire voyage of the *Freya* would have been in the Pacific Ocean. That means that the *Freya* was lost in the Pacific, not the Atlantic.

Not only did Lawrence Kusche place the loss of the *Freya* an ocean away from the Bermuda Triangle, he also found a likely explanation for the ship's loss.

That likely explanation was part of an article in the April 25, 1907, issue of *Nature,* a British science magazine. According to the article, a series of earthquakes shook the west coast of Mexico shortly after the *Freya* sailed out of Manzanillo harbor on October 3, 1902.

Twenty days later, the *Freya* was found. The ship was crewless and battered. It was floating on its side near Mazatlán, another port on the west coast of Mexico.

What happened to the *Freya*? At first, no one could answer that question, for there had been no storms in the area.

However, according to the *Nature* article, a marked calendar in the captain's cabin aboard the *Freya* provided a clue to the ship's fate. It seemed that the captain marked off the days as they passed. The last date marked on the calendar was October 4.

Earthquake tremors were felt up and down the west coast of Mexico on October 4 and October 5, 1902. It's quite likely that these earthquakes shook up part of the nearby sea floor as well as the land. In that case, an undersea earthquake or "seaquake" could produce a mighty tidal wave that might flip the ship over on its side and wash the crew overboard. At least, that was the opinion of the writers of the 1907 *Nature* article.

There will always be some doubt about the fate of the *Freya.* But there can be no doubt that the *Freya* was lost far away from the Bermuda Triangle.

Why then was the *Freya* listed as a Bermuda Triangle victim?

Lawrence Kusche figures that sometime in the past someone made a mistake and listed the ship's port of departure as Manzanillo, Cuba. If that had been the ship's port of departure, the *Freya* would have sailed somewhat close to the Bermuda Triangle area on the first leg of its voyage to Chile. It was on that basis that the *Freya* was listed as a Bermuda Triangle victim in book after book. None of the Bermuda Triangle authors, except Lawrence Kusche, seems to have checked the facts on the actual course of the *Freya*.

That, Mr. Kusche contends, is a typical example of the careless research that created the Bermuda Triangle mystery in the first place. If authors had checked the facts on all the supposed Bermuda Triangle victims, Mr. Kusche argues, there would be no mystery. In his opinion, many of the ship and plane disappearances that did occur in or near the Bermuda Triangle can be explained by natural causes and/or human error.

As an example, Mr. Kusche gives the case of a DC-3 passenger plane that disappeared on December 28, 1948. The plane was on a flight from San Juan, Puerto Rico, to Miami, Florida.

Many, but not all, of the Bermuda Triangle mystery books say that the DC-3 airliner vanished for no apparent reason in beautiful weather within sight of Miami. According to these accounts, the airliner's crew was having no difficulties. The flight had been perfect. One minute the pilot was asking for landing instructions at Miami, and the next minute there was complete silence. The DC-3 vanished without warning and without leaving a trace.

Lawrence Kusche read the accident investigation report prepared by the Civil Aeronautics Board (CAB). In that report, Mr. Kusche discovered that all had not been well with that DC-3. There were definite difficulties.

Right from the start of the flight, the airliner's radio equipment had not been working right. The plane's crew was never in direct contact with the Miami control tower. Radio messages between the plane and Miami had to be relayed through an air traffic control station in New Orleans, Louisiana.

That's not all. When the airliner took off from San Juan, its batteries were known to be bad. Furthermore, mechanics checking the plane for the flight found signs of trouble in the plane's electrical system. The pilot was told about these defects, but he decided to take off anyway.

Civil Aeronautics Board investigators figured that the plane's electrical system may have failed completely during the flight. If that happened, the plane's radio and compass and other instruments were made useless. Then the pilot would have been unable to find his way or contact anyone. About seven and one-half hours after takeoff, long past sunset, the plane would have run out of fuel. Then the pilot would have had no choice but to ditch the plane in a dark,

Around Bermuda the sea surface can change from calm to rough and dangerous with surprising suddenness. Here, an 80 knot gale whips up the ocean surface. (*U.S. Navy*)

dangerous, shark infested sea. It is also quite possible that the plane would have quickly sunk into deep water without leaving a trace.

Of course there is no proof that that is what actually happened. Since the wreckage of the DC-3 was never found, no one will ever know whether or not the airliner's electrical system failed. CAB investigators decided that they could not determine the probable cause of the DC-3 airliner's disappearance.

Lawrence Kusche agrees that the exact cause of the DC-3 loss will never be known. But he points out that the plane was having difficulties that could account for the loss, and that most Bermuda Triangle mystery writers overlooked those difficulties. In Mr. Kusche's opinion, the circumstances of the airliner's disappearance are not nearly so mysterious as most writers make out.

There are, however, some total sea and sky mysteries in the area. Mr. Kusche could not find any possible cause for the disappearances of the ship HMS *Atalanta,* and of the airliners *Star Tiger* and *Star Ariel.*

Some of the likely causes that Mr. Kusche has suggested for the disappearances of other ships and planes can be challenged. For instance, Mr. Kusche strongly believes that the PBM flying boat that was lost while searching for missing Flight 19 in December, 1945, exploded in midair. There's evidence to support this belief. Crew members of the merchant ship S.S. *Gaines Mills* saw and heard an explosion in the sky near the place where the PBM Mariner should have been at that time. The flying boat seems to have exploded in midair, but why would it have exploded in midair?

Mr. Kusche offers a "plausible" explanation. He says that PBM "Mariners were nicknamed 'flying gas tanks' because of the fumes that were often present. A crewman sneaking a cigarette, or a spark from any source, could have caused the explosion."

Many people have trouble accepting that explanation. I am one of them. As a U.S. Air Force radio operator, I flew on U.S. Navy PBM flying boats a few times in 1952 and 1953. During those times, I never heard of the planes being called "flying gas tanks." I never noticed gasoline fumes within the aircraft. It also seems extremely unlikely that a crew member would sneak a cigarette during a rescue mission. Since the 1950s, I have talked to other people who flew on PBM's, and they never mentioned the nickname, "flying gas tank."

Furthermore, PBM flying boats were extensively used by the U.S. Navy over a long period of time. Would the Navy have used PBM-type aircraft so frequently if the planes were known to have a deadly flaw that could cause them to explode in midair?

Some of Lawrence Kusche's remarks on the loss of Flight 19 can also be questioned. Most of the Bermuda Triangle mystery writers insist that the pilots of Flight 19 were experienced. Mr. Kusche disagrees. He calls the pilots "students." This gives the impression that the pilots were learning to fly. Mr. Kusche points out that the pilots were on a "training mission." In fact, however, the Navy considered the pilots to be "qualified." They were engaged in an advanced, overwater navigation training course.

It is obvious, as Mr. Kusche points out, that the pilots of Flight 19 were confused and lost. Mr. Kusche blames the flight's difficulties on the failure of Lt. Taylor's compass and Lt. Taylor's confusion over time and place. But there seems to be more to it than that. The total disappearance of Flight 19 continues to be one of the great air mysteries of all times. It is a key part of the "Bermuda Triangle mystery."

Has Lawrence Kusche finally solved the Bermuda Triangle mystery? He has indeed solved parts of the mystery. He has shortened the list of Bermuda Triangle victims, and has offered many likely explanations for some of the mysteries. Perhaps most of all, he has exposed errors and faulty conclusions that had crept into the accounts of ship and plane disappearances.

But many mysteries still remain.

Chapter 8

WHERE STORMS ARE BORN

"My research, which began as an attempt to find as much information as possible about the Bermuda Triangle, had an unexpected result," Lawrence Kusche declares in *The Bermuda Triangle Mystery—Solved.* "After examining all the evidence I have reached the following conclusion: *There is no theory that solves the mystery.*"

Mr. Kusche adds: "It is no more logical to try to find a common cause for all the disappearances in the Triangle than, for example, to try to find one cause for all the automobile accidents in Arizona."

That statement demands some thought.

Suppose that Arizona has a higher rate of automobile accidents than other states. In that case, wouldn't it be logical to look for some common cause, or causes, for most of the automobile accidents in Arizona?

It might turn out that road construction and road maintenance in Arizona were contributing factors to the high accident rate. Road sign design could also be a contributing cause. Weather conditions in sections of the state might be partly to blame for the high accident rate. Rules and tests for drivers' licences and car registrations might be part of the problem.

It can make sense to look for common causes to help explain a rash of automobile accidents on land. Therefore, wouldn't it make equal sense to look for common causes to help explain a rash of ship and plane disappearances in a particular patch of ocean?

Certain features of the atmosphere and ocean might be such "common causes." These features may make one area of ocean much more dangerous than other areas. Sailors have always known this. The conditions that make certain ocean areas particularly dangerous may not be a mystery. Driving gales, shifting sands, and frequent fog can be blamed for ship losses in such dangerous sea areas as the Strait of Magellan, the off-shore vicinity of Cape Hatteras, North Carolina, and the Grand Banks off the coast of Newfoundland.

There's seldom a mystery about ship losses in those areas. The hazards are fairly obvious. Danger tends to come with some warning, and resulting wreckage is often found.

That is not the case with all hazardous ocean areas. There is at least one area where danger often comes *without* warning. The source of the danger can be so localized that no one but the victims may be aware of it when it actually strikes.

In that hazardous ocean area, ships and planes may completely vanish. Wreckage is seldom found. Each loss is shrouded in mystery.

One such hazardous ocean area ranges from the Gulf of Mexico to a point in the mid-Atlantic northeast of Bermuda. The area also extends southward into the Caribbean Sea. This hazardous ocean area encloses the Bermuda Triangle. To some people, the entire area is the Bermuda Triangle.

There are many natural hazards in this region of the sea. These hazards are complex and varied, and they are not always easy to identify. Winds may blow gently one minute, then fiercely the next. They frequently shift in their directions.

Hurricanes are "born" in the area. So are waterspouts—tiny relatives of the big storms.

Violent atmospheric storms come and go in the night with savage suddenness. In this area, the clear-skied peace of a summer day is often broken by the explosive growth of a towering thundercloud. Far beneath the waves hidden storms may often rage.

In this particularly stormy and changeable patch of ocean, ship and plane losses can be sudden, surprising, and total. Frequently, there are no calls for help, no survivors, no bodies, and no wreckage. A ship may sail into a calm sea under a cloudless sky—then vanish. A plane may disappear there after reporting that "all is well."

No wonder a legend has developed about the area. Is it surprising that this patch of ocean continues to frighten and fascinate people? Is it surprising that there is a Bermuda Triangle mystery?

Christopher Columbus sailed into this treacherous area during his voyage of discovery in 1492. The great explorer did not, however, find the area very hazardous on that occasion. Years later, Columbus must have realized how lucky he was on his first voyage to the New World.

Columbus's ships—*Nina, Pinta, Santa Maria*—sailed westward through the Atlantic Ocean during August, September, and early October of 1492. At that time of year, hurricanes were raging in the western Atlantic. Of course Columbus didn't know that. He was completely unaware of the ship-shattering storms that were in his path. Luckily, the storms had moved out of his path by the time the three tiny ships sailed into the area south of Bermuda.

Many times on later voyages, Columbus tempted fate by sailing in the western Atlantic during the hurricane season. But his luck held—until the summer of 1502. Then, the weather luck of Christopher Columbus started to run out.

Computer drawing shows how air particles swirl around in a hurricane. (*NOAA*)

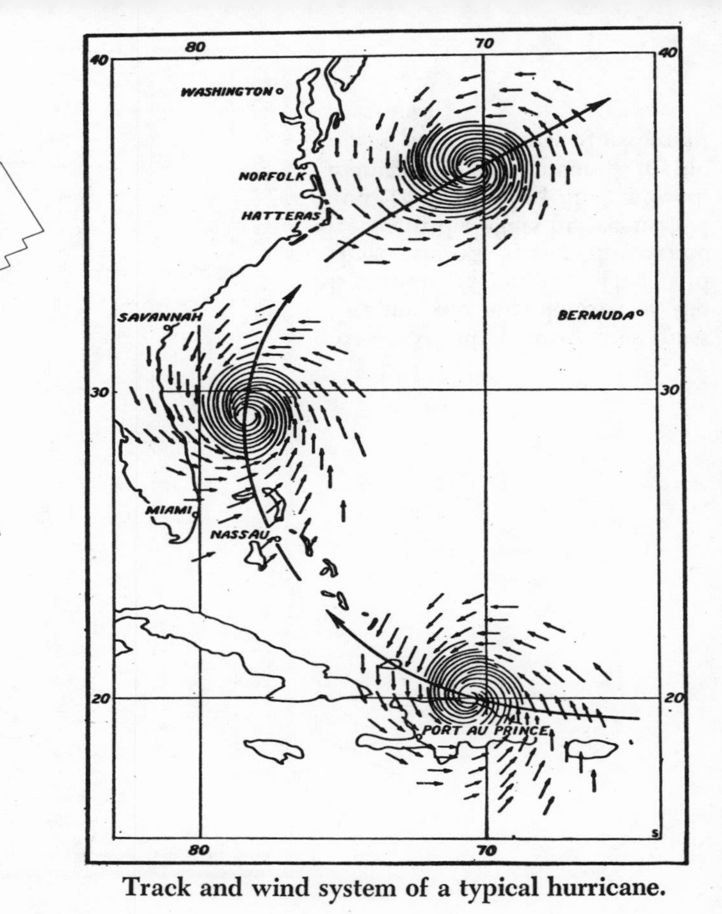

Track and wind system of a typical hurricane.

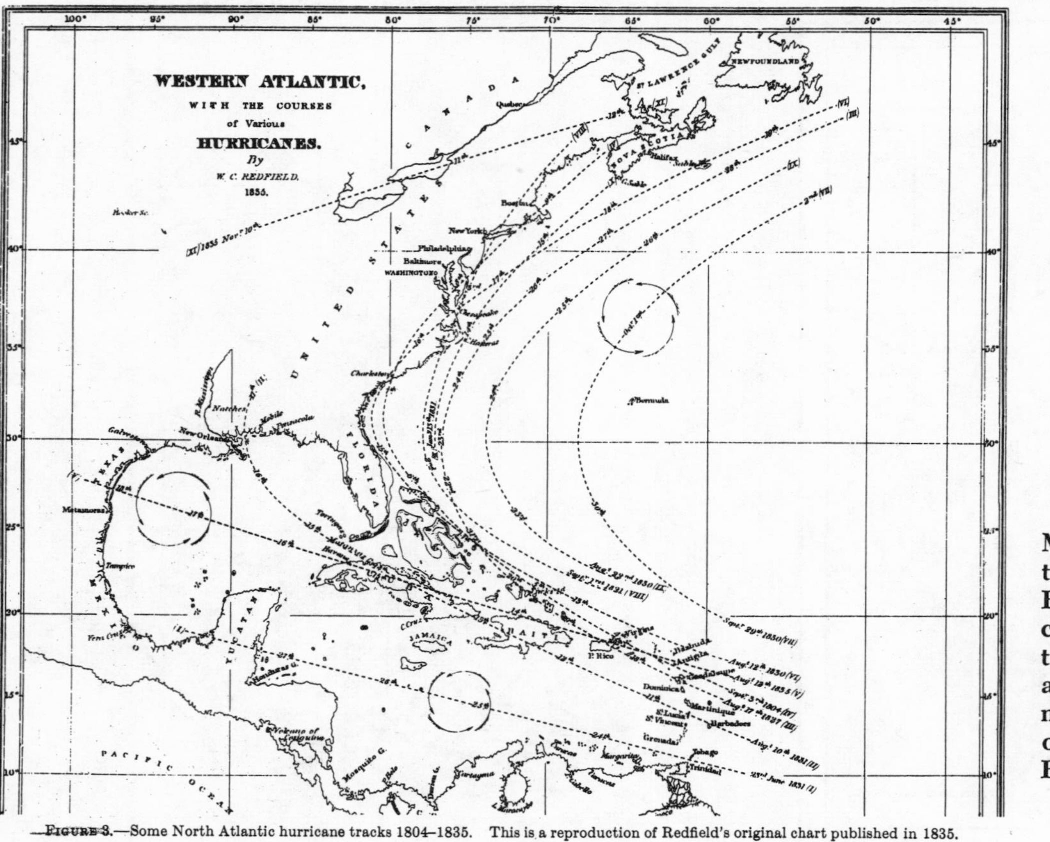

FIGURE 3.—Some North Atlantic hurricane tracks 1804–1835. This is a reproduction of Redfield's original chart published in 1835.

Most Atlantic hurricanes pass through the area known as the Bermuda Triangle. This old chart shows major hurricane tracks in the years between 1804 and 1835. During that period, many ships disappeared in the ocean area between Florida and Bermuda.

By 1502, Columbus was well aware of hurricanes. He had developed a keen "weather eye" for signs that such a storm was developing. In June 1502, Columbus saw the weather signs of a coming hurricane. As a result he tried to shelter his ships in the harbor of Santo Domingo (the present capital of the Dominican Republic) on the island of Hispaniola. Columbus also advised the Governor of Santo Domingo to delay the sailing of a treasure fleet of thirty ships bound for Spain.

The governor of Santo Domingo didn't like Columbus, so he refused to allow Columbus's ships to stay in the harbor. He wouldn't delay the sailing of the treasure fleet either.

Columbus found shelter in a small harbor. When the hurricane struck, his ships were only lightly damaged. But the treasure fleet was not so lucky. It ran into the hurricane. As a result, 26 ships and more than 500 persons were lost. Very little treasure from the New World reached Spain that year.

When the storm damage to Columbus's ships was repaired, the little fleet sailed southward to explore Caribbean islands. Late in the year, near the coast of Panama, Columbus encountered two more examples of the dangerous weather of the tropical seas.

Fierce winds and towering waves battered Columbus's ships. Torrents of rain poured down. Flashes of lightning threatened the wood and canvas ships with fire.

Columbus called this storm a tempest. While the tempest raged, a "dangerous and wonderful" waterspout passed between two of the ships. Though the waterspout did no damage, the ships' crews were terrified.

Two years later, on his last long voyage home, Columbus ran into the worst weather of his sea-going career. A hurricane swept away the main mast of the ship Columbus was on. The crew rigged a makeshift mast. A few days later, another storm swept that mast away. From then on it was slow sailing for Columbus. It seemed as if the stormy sea wanted to keep the "admiral of the ocean sea."

From old accounts, it seems that Columbus first encountered a hurricane and then a tropical storm on his last voyage. Actually a hurricane and a tropical storm are the same type of atmospheric disturbance. They are both tropical cyclones or "whirling wind storms."

A tropical cyclone of a certain size and wind speed is called a "hurricane" in the Atlantic Ocean. Tropical cyclones are known by different names in other ocean areas of the world—"typhoons" in the Pacific, "cyclones" in the Indian Ocean, and "willy-willies" in the seas near Australia.

All of these storms form over patches of particularly warm water. Tropical disturbances form over tropical seas usually at certain times of the year. In the tropical region of the Atlantic there is a hurricane season. This usually occurs when the sun is directly overhead. Water evaporates rapidly from a patch of warm sea surface. As the warm, moisture-laden air rises from the surface of the patch of sea, cooler, denser air swirls in to take the place of the rising air. As the cool air spirals in, it is warmed. That air also rises. As time passes, the process speeds up—warm air rises, cool air swirls in to take its place, that air is heated, it rises faster than before, more air swirls in, and so on.

As the moisture-laden air rises, it cools and condenses. Rain drops fall and heat energy is released. This energy feeds the storm. Eventually the result is a raging hurricane.

Meteorologists (weather scientists) tend to reserve the name "hurricane" for tropical cyclones whose winds exceed sixty-five knots (almost seventy-five miles per hour). Below that wind velocity, the cyclones are known as "tropical storms."

The hurricane season runs from July through October with most hurricanes occurring during August and September. The sun shines directly on the region during June and July

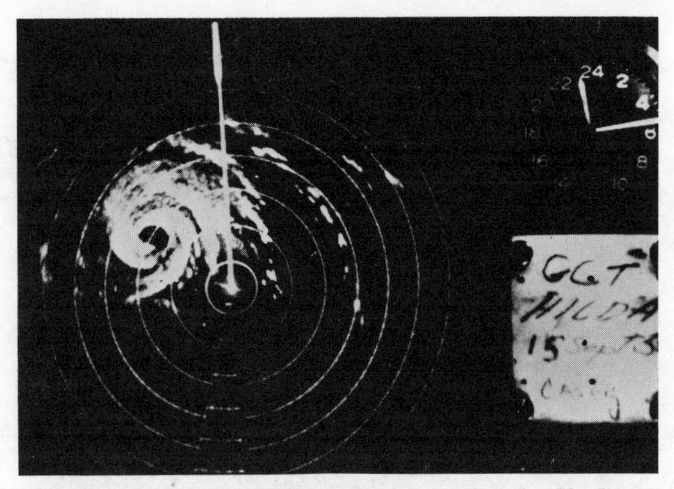

A radar plot reveals the spiral shape of a deadly hurricane. (*U.S. Weather Bureau*)

Looking down into a hurricane from an altitude of 20,000 feet. (*U.S. Weather Bureau*)

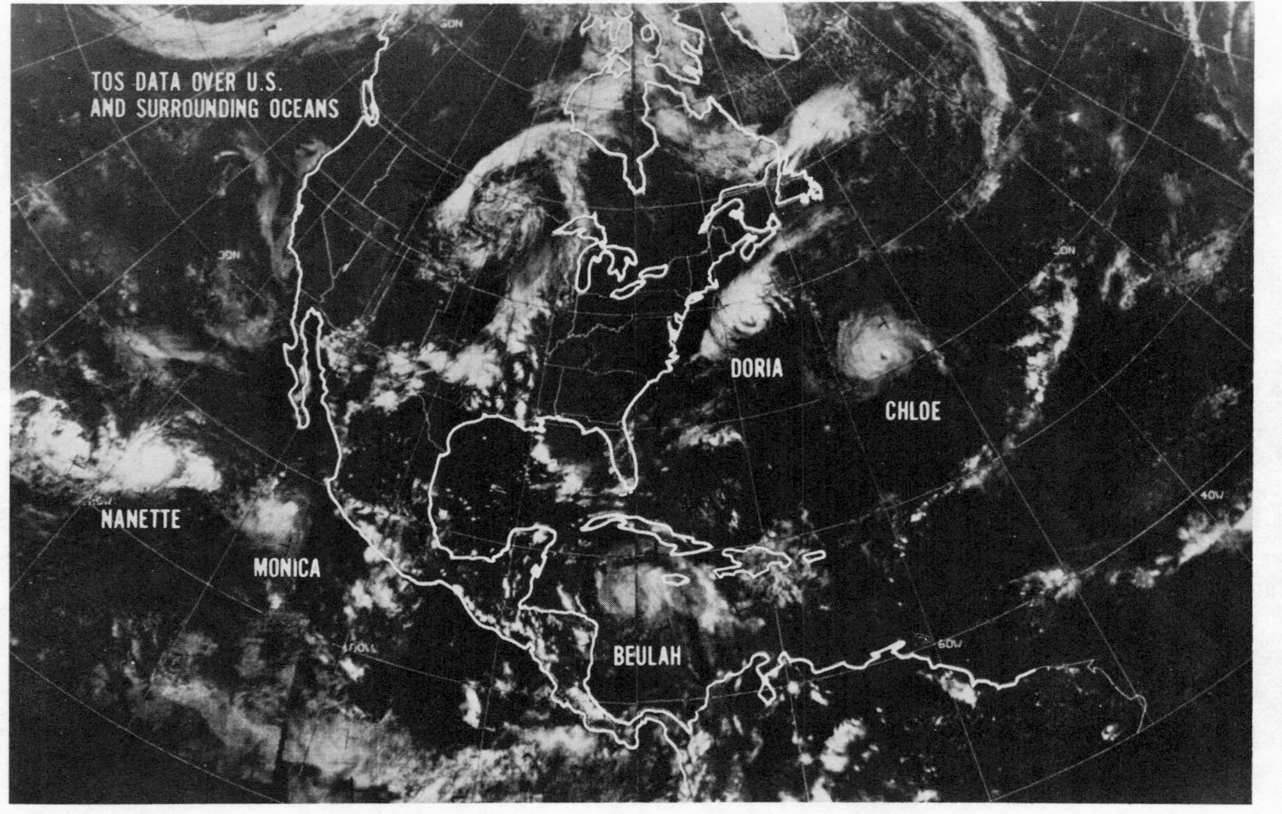

Photos taken by a weather satellite on September 14, 1967, show three hurricanes in the western Atlantic region at the same time. (*NOAA*)

and during September and October. Therefore, the sea surface there should be warmest at those times. But that isn't always the case. There are other influences at work.

Ocean currents move warm and cold water around on and near the ocean surface. At the same time, vertical currents, known as "ocean elevators," lift cold water from the ocean depths to sections of the ocean surface. What's more, winds blowing over the ocean tend to cool some surface areas more than others. Even the shape of nearby land masses can influence surface water temperature.

We would expect a band of ocean receiving the same amount of sunlight to have the same water temperature across its surface. But, owing to the influences of winds and ocean currents, that is not so. Some patches of tropical sea surface are warmer than others.

All hurricanes develop in the tropical Atlantic north of the equator. Some hurricanes and tropical storms form in the eastern Atlantic near the Cape Verde Islands. Most hurricanes, however, develop in the western tropical Atlantic around the West Indies, and in the nearby Caribbean Sea and Gulf of Mexico.

The great mass of air over the North Atlantic Ocean circulates very slowly in a clockwise direction. This mass of air is like a huge wheel turning. Hurricanes form at the "bottom rim of this wheel," and they move around with the "rim." As a result, Cape Verde hurricanes at first travel westward toward the West Indies, and then they swing northwestward toward the United States coastline. West Indies hurricanes usually travel northwestward or, in some cases, directly northward toward the U.S. coast.

The winds of hurricanes and all tropical cyclones in the northern hemisphere swirl around in a counterclockwise direction. But the hurricanes themselves tend to travel in a clockwise direction. This clockwise movement of hurricanes tends to take most of them through the Bermuda Triangle.

Some hurricanes are actually "born" in the Triangle. Many tropical storms that don't reach hurricane status "die" there. As a result, the Bermuda Triangle is an area of frequent storms. Surely that is a common cause that may help explain some of the ship and plane disappearances in that area of ocean.

Chapter 9

THE OCEAN RIVER AND THE SEAWEED SEA

In the tropical regions of the Atlantic Ocean, the trade winds blow all the time.

North of the equator, the prevailing tropical winds blow from the northeast. Cool, relatively dry air flows southwestward from the vicinity of the European land mass. Curving down past the wide bulge of North Africa, this flow of air is turned westward by a force resulting from the rotation of the earth. In the days of sail, ships took advantage of this constant air flow to speed their voyages to the New World. As a result, this flow of air was named the *northeast trade winds.*

South of the equator, there is a similar wind pattern. In that tropical region, air flows from the southeast. It blows in a northwesterly direction up the African coast. Then, that air flow is also turned westward by a force resulting from the earth's rotation. This air flow south of the equator is known as the *southeast trade winds.*

Sandwiched between the northeast trade winds and the southeast trade winds is an area where a strong wind seldom blows. This area of calm straddles the equator and stretches around the globe. It is known as the *doldrums.*

In the doldrums, the sea surface is usually calm, the sky is usually clear. In the old days, sailing ships might be stranded there for weeks without a puff of wind to fill their sails.

North and south of the doldrums, the trade winds often howl. Sailors would look forward to a sometimes rough passage in the zones of the trade winds. As they blow, these strong winds force masses of ocean-surface water westward toward the Americas.

In the northern hemisphere, the constantly flowing mass of water that is "pushed" westward by the northeast trade winds is called the *North Equatorial Current.* In the southern hemisphere, a similar flow of water is called the *South Equatorial Current.* Both of these ocean currents influence weather conditions and sea conditions in the western tropical region of the Atlantic. Both of these currents may be indirectly responsible for some plane and ship losses in the Bermuda Triangle area.

North and south of the equator, these currents of water become warmer as they flow westward through the warm tropical regions of the Atlantic Ocean. These currents also tend to flow faster as they approach the Americas. Not only are the currents "pushed along" by the trade winds, they are also "pulled along" by a force resulting from earth's rotation.

Warm and swift, the North Equatorial Current flows around the islands of the West Indies. As it does so, the main current is split into two branch currents by the chain of islands. One branch current swings northward, on the outside of the islands, toward Florida. This branch is often called the *Windward Current.* It is also known as the *Antilles Current.*

The other branch of the North Equatorial Current flows south of the West Indies into the Caribbean Sea. That branch current is called the *Caribbean Current.*

In the Caribbean Sea, a meeting of waters occurs. The southern branch of the North Equatorial Current merges with the northern branch of the South Equatorial Current.

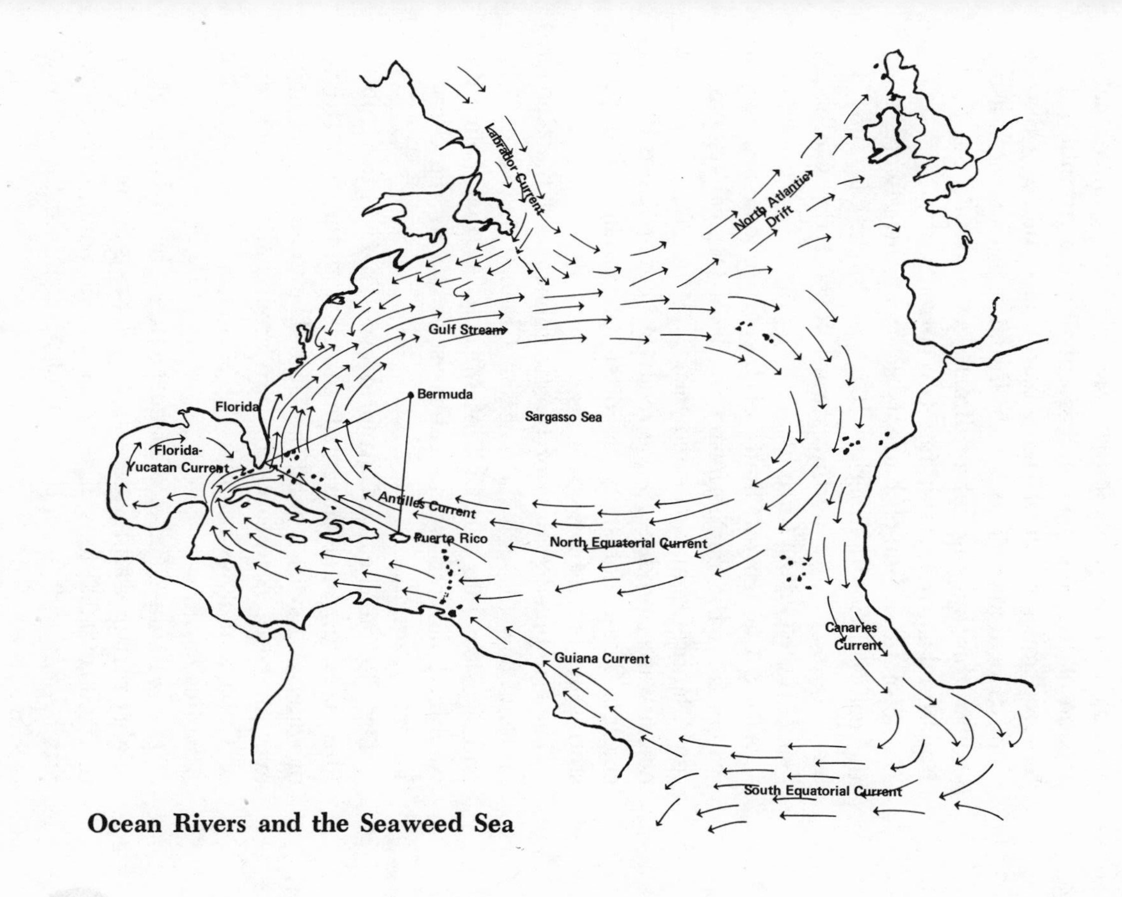

Ocean Rivers and the Seaweed Sea

The combined waters of the two branch currents flow into the Gulf of Mexico.

Look at a map of South America. You'll notice that a section of the continent bulges out into the Atlantic a few hundred miles south of the equator. That bulge is Brazil's Cape São Roque. The South Equatorial Current washes against this bulging bit of Brazil. As a result, the South Equatorial Current is split into two currents.

One of these branch currents flows southwestward along the coast of South America. It is the *Brazil Current*. The other branch flows northwestward toward the Caribbean Sea. It is the *Guiana Current*.

Within the narrow limits of the Caribbean Sea, warm waters from the northern and southern tropical regions of the Atlantic Ocean meet and mix. This merging of tropical ocean waters produces some relatively hot spots on the sea surface. These hot spots are often the cradles of tropical storms and hurricanes.

The combined waters of the Caribbean and the Guiana currents flow through the Yucatan Channel, between Cuba and Mexico, into the Gulf of Mexico. At that point, the combined flow of warm waters is known as the *Florida-Yucatan Current*.

The Florida-Yucatan Current doesn't linger in the Gulf of Mexico. A few small currents break off from the main stream of water and swirl around the Gulf. The main stream, however, makes a northeastward turn around the western end of Cuba and flows through the Straits of Florida into the Atlantic Ocean.

The Florida-Yucatan Current enters the Atlantic as a mighty rush of warm water. Ocean scientists figure that close to 90,000,000,000 tons of water a minute pour through the Straits of Florida from the Gulf of Mexico into the Atlantic Ocean.

This mighty rush of water through the Straits sets up swirling currents that can be dangerous to boats and small ships sailing among the Florida Keys. In addition, the interaction of the warm waters of the Florida-Yucatan Current with the colder waters of the Atlantic Ocean produces frequent fog in and near the Florida Straits.

Tricky currents, frequent fog, and sudden storms make the Florida Straits a dangerous area for sailors and a favorite hunting ground for treasure divers. A Spanish galleon loaded with gold and silver sank there in 1765. In 1711, an entire Spanish treasure fleet was lost in the Straits.

Beyond. the treacherous Florida Straits, the emerging waters of the Florida-Yucatan Current meet and mix with the very warm waters of the Antilles (Windward) Current. The result is the great *Gulf Stream.*

Viewed from space, the Gulf Stream appears as a dark-blue river snaking northeastward off the coast of Florida. The Gulf Stream is in a sense a river, a mighty river of warm

The Gulf Stream can often be seen from aircraft flying eastward over the ocean from Florida. (*Woods Hole Oceanographic Institution*)

water flowing through the cold blue-green ocean. No river on land can match this ocean river. Ten times more water flows in the Gulf Stream than in the Mississippi River.

North by northeast, the Gulf Stream flows up past the coastlines of Florida, Georgia, South Carolina, and North Carolina. Off the shore of North Carolina, in the vicinity of Cape Hatteras, the northward-flowing warm waters of the Gulf Stream clash with the southward-flowing cold waters of the "dying" *Labrador Current* (dying because it is slowing down, becoming warmer, and losing its distinctiveness).

This meeting of warm and cold ocean currents is often stormy enough to make Cape Hatteras a major threat to Atlantic shipping. Sudden storms and shifting sands turn the area into a sailor's nightmare.

The wreck-strewn sands and shoals of Cape Hatteras mark the end of the line for the Labrador Current, and a turning point for the Gulf Stream. Buffeted by the inshore flow of the Labrador Current, the Gulf Stream is diverted, swinging northeastward into the wide Atlantic Ocean.

Northeastward, then eastward, the Gulf Stream flows across the Atlantic. It is pushed along by the prevailing winds which are known as the *westerlies,* or *anti-trades.*

As it flows toward Europe, the Gulf Stream loses some warmth, some blueness, and much distinctiveness. In the eastern North Atlantic, the Gulf Stream no longer stands out bold and blue against the grey-blue-green expanse of ocean. Even from the vantage point of an earth-orbiting spacecraft, the Gulf Stream can't easily be distinguished from the surrounding sea.

At a point north and west of the Azores, the Gulf Stream comes apart. Part of the Stream, the *North Atlantic Drift,* continues to drift toward Europe. The other branch swings southeastward around the Azores, then southward past the Canary Islands. That branch is then called the *Canaries Current.*

Crewmen of the U.S. Coast Guard patrol ship lower an STD (salinity, temperature, depth) sensor into the Atlantic Ocean east of Florida. Measurements provided by such instruments enable oceanographers to track the ever-changing Gulf Stream. (*U.S. Coast Guard*)

South of the Canary Islands, the Canaries Current is turned westward by a force resulting from the earth's rotation. The northeast trade winds nudge the flow of water westward. That flow becomes part of the North Equatorial Current, moving west to renew the Gulf Stream.

Round and round the currents go in the North Atlantic, forming a gyre (a circular flow of water). Within this gyre is a calm sea area, partly covered with sea weeds known as sargassum. The sea without a shore is called the *Sargasso Sea.*

The Sargasso Sea is a lens-shaped, shallow mass of warm, very salty water resting on a cold ocean. It is ringed and trapped by a circular flow of ocean currents. These currents flow swiftly in the west and lazily in the east. Without a doubt, the Gulf Stream is the most influential of these currents. Some people call the whole circular system of currents the Gulf Stream.

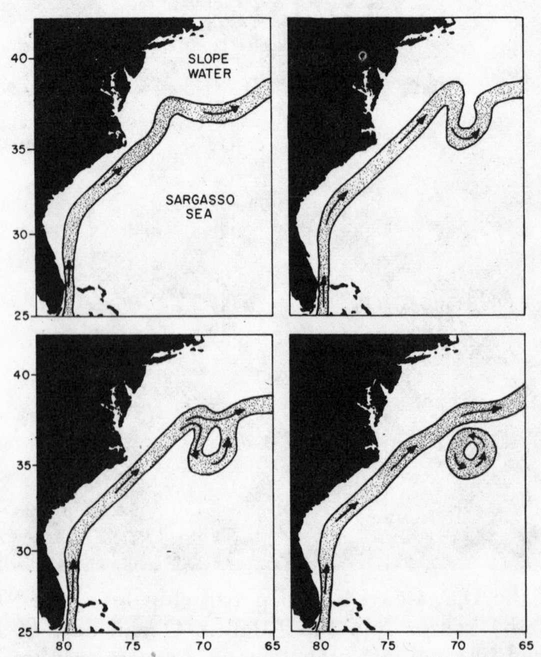

Every once in a while, currents of warm water break away from the Gulf Stream. These break-away currents are called eddies. They swirl around for a time and are then absorbed by the ocean. Four drawings based on measurements made by the U.S. Naval Oceanographic Office in 1970 show how a Gulf Stream eddy is formed. (*University of Rhode Island*)

Most of the Sargasso Sea is located in a section of the ocean where few strong winds blow. This band of relative calm is known as the *horse latitudes.* (Sailing ships carrying horses to the New World were often becalmed for days in those latitudes. When food for the horses ran out, the horses were thrown overboard, or had to be eaten because the crew had run out of food—hence, the name.)

The horse latitudes are sandwiched between the northeast trade winds to the south and the westerlies in the north. Christopher Columbus sailed into the horse latitudes in 1492. For a time, his three ships made little progress. Then, west of the Azores, Columbus saw seaweed floating in the water. He thought he was near land since seaweed is usually found close to shore. But he wasn't near land. Columbus had entered the Sargasso Sea.

Sargassum (also called gulfweed—a type of brown algae), the floating weeds, seem to have completely adapted to life in the warm mass of very salty water held in by the circular system of ocean currents in the mid-Atlantic. The weeds are thickest at the western end of the Sargasso Sea. That is where the ocean currents flow swiftest, and where the trapped waters of the Sargasso Sea are warmest.

Many legends have developed about the Sargasso Sea. Old sailors used to say that the weeds there were thick enough to grab and hold a ship for ever. The area has been called the "graveyard of lost ships." Sailors also swore that monsters lived among the thick seaweeds.

Since the Sargasso Sea extends well into the area known as the Bermuda Triangle, some Sargasso Sea legends have been mixed with stories of the Bermuda Triangle mystery. Writers have described the Sargasso Sea as a strange, frightening, mysterious place, teeming with life.

Recent scientific studies have, however, shown that the Sargasso Sea is not very mysterious, not very frightening, and definitely not teeming with life. Nowhere are the weeds so thick that they might slow the movement of a ship; nor is the sea strewn with the remains of stranded ships. In the days of sail, ships were often kept motionless for days in the Sargasso Sea. But that was due to the windless condition of the horse latitudes in general. To sailors on the becalmed ships, however, the weeds floating all around may have seemed responsible for the ships' lack of progress.

Weeds floating on the Sargasso Sea led explorers and sailors to think that the sea was full of living things. Nothing could be further from the truth. Scientists have discovered that the Sargasso Sea is almost a biological desert. Less plankton—the tiny plants and animals that form the base of the ocean food chain—is found in the Sargasso Sea than elsewhere. The Sargasso Sea has the lowest plankton count in the world. It seems that the warm salty conditions that encourage the floating seaweed to grow may discourage the reproduction of plankton.

The Gulf Stream and other currents encircle and entrap a large patch of calm, relatively warm water on the ocean surface around Bermuda. Weeds known as sargassum float on the water and give the area its name—the Sargasso Sea. Old sailors believed that the weeds were so thick there that ships could be held in the sargassum weeds' grip. As a result, the legend of the Sargasso Sea became part of the legend of the Bermuda Triangle. (*University of Rhode Island*)

The amount of plankton in the Sargasso Sea varies from place to place and from time to time. So does the amount of seaweed floating on the sea. No one has yet established a firm link between the two. No one can say for certain that each rise in the amount of plankton is matched by a fall in the amount of seaweed, or vice versa.

Scientists have noticed, however, that the density of the floating weeds is influenced by changes in the temperature, salinity, size, shape, and position of the Sargasso Sea. These changes in the Sargasso Sea are influenced, in turn, by changes in the Gulf Stream and its related currents swirling around the Sargasso Sea.

For years scientists have realized that the Gulf Stream is not steady and unchanging. Its temperature, direction of flow, and speed vary from hour-to-hour, day-to-day, and month-to-month.

As the moon passes over the ocean, it pulls on the currents and alters their flow. In other words, variations in the flow of the Gulf Stream are related to ocean tides. The seasons of the year, changes in air pressure, surface storms, and storms far beneath the surface of the sea also cause changes in the character and flow of the Gulf Stream.

Scientists are very interested in variations of the Gulf Stream because these variations influence the weather throughout the entire North Atlantic region. The flow of heat from the warm waters of the Gulf Stream into the cool air above greatly influences the circulation of the atmosphere. Therefore, changes in the Gulf Stream produce changes in the atmosphere, and, to a lesser extent, changes in the atmosphere produce changes in the Gulf Stream.

In the western tropical region of the Atlantic, the Gulf Stream flows fast, warm, and deep. As it flows between Florida and the Bahamas the Gulf Stream is about 48 miles wide and 440 fathoms (2640 feet) deep. In that area, it is truly an ocean river. Farther to the north, the Gulf Stream is much wider, shallower and cooler.

Where it flows fastest, warmest, and deepest, the Gulf Stream has great influence on the weather. As a result, every sudden change, every spin-off current, every wobble in this mighty ocean river can produce weather peculiarities (called variables) in the area. These peculiar weather conditions may have been partly responsible for the mysterious disappearances of many ships and planes in the ocean region east of Florida, south of Bermuda, and north of the West Indies.

Scientists are studying oceanic and atmospheric phenomena of the western tropical region of the Atlantic. Might their studies solve parts of the Bermuda Triangle mystery?

Yes! But the scientists won't admit to having anything to do with the Bermuda Triangle mystery. It has a bad name in scientific circles.

Chapter 10
SCIENCE AND SEA MYSTERIES

What strange forces are at work in the Bermuda Triangle?

Are time, space, magnetism, and gravity mixed up in that ocean area?

What happened to all the ships, planes, and people that vanished there?

Will science ever solve the mystery of the Bermuda Triangle?

Those questions, particularly the last one, are almost guaranteed to make scientists angry.

"Bermuda Triangle? There's no such place!" is the usual reply.

Scientists, oceanographers, and meteorologists in particular are sick and tired of all the fuss about a Bermuda Triangle mystery. "Nonsense," they say, to talk of space time warps. "Double-nonsense," they say, to talk of flying saucer invaders from another world.

The scientists view each loss as a single, separate tragedy. If the facts were known, they say, each loss could be explained in terms of natural events, human error, mechanical failure, or some combination of all three.

Scientists point out that about 350 ships a year are lost throughout the world, and several of those ships disappear without warning and without leaving a trace. "Many sections of the world's oceans could," the scientists say, "be labeled mystery zones."

While denying that there is a "Bermuda Triangle," many scientists consider the tropical ocean area bounded by Bermuda, Florida, and the West Indies to be somewhat unique. The area has some peculiar ocean and weather conditions. The scientists agree that these conditions could be responsible for many of the ship and plane losses in the area.

Though they are unwilling to talk about the Bermuda Triangle mystery, scientists are, in a sense, solving that mystery. They are solving it by gaining an understanding of the oceanic and meteorologic phenomena peculiar to the western tropical region of the Atlantic Ocean. Studies of ocean and weather peculiarities can provide general clues to the fates of those ships and planes. As scientific knowledge of the area increases, the mysteries of the area are bound to become less mysterious.

One significant ocean phenomenon of the area was discovered quite by chance in 1959. At that time, British oceanographer John Swallow was trying to measure the flow of deep currents in the western Atlantic. To do that, Dr. Swallow was using floats designed to drift freely at various fixed depths beneath the ocean surface. (Those devices are now known as Swallow floats.)

One by one, Dr. Swallow launched his floats. Using special instruments the scientist tracked the floats. Some of the deep water floats drifted as expected. But others swirled off in unexpected directions at unusual speeds. The "wrong-way" floats drifted about ten times faster than expected. It seemed to Dr. Swallow that his runaway floats were in the grasp of underwater whirlpools. And, in a way, they were. Dr. Swallow had discovered deep-water eddies.

Eddies are swift, swirling currents of water that seem to break away from major ocean currents. There are upper-layer eddies that occur on or near the ocean surface, and there are, as Dr. Swallow discovered, deep-water eddies that can occur thousands of feet beneath the waves.

Upper-layer eddies tend to pack more energy than their deep-water relatives. However, the deep water eddies seem to be more erratic and changeable than the upper-layer variety. Furthermore, deep-water eddies may be a factor in undersea storms. Undersea storms are violent movements of water layers in the ocean depths that may be a threat to deep-diving submarines.

Eddies occur throughout most of the world's oceans. But the western tropical region of the Atlantic seems to have more of these ocean whirlpools than any place else.

In 1971, University of Rhode Island oceanographers aboard the research vessel *Trident* observed highly energetic eddies spin away from the Gulf Stream into the Sargasso Sea. Within the Sargasso Sea, the eddies seemed to wander aim-

Ocean scientists and weather scientists teamed up to conduct many careful studies of the tropical region of the North Atlantic during the 1960s and 1970s. Here, ships, planes, and weather balloons are used to measure and relate sea states and atmospheric conditions. (*U.S. Coast and Geodetic Survey*)

lessly. As they wandered, they gave up considerable amounts of energy to the atmosphere and to the surrounding ocean waters.

For years scientists have wondered how and where eddies form. Why do they follow certain paths? How do they interact with each other? How do they interact with ocean currents? How do they interact with the atmosphere? How much energy do ocean eddies transfer to the atmosphere?

In 1970, a group of scientists from the Massachusetts Institute of Technology (MIT) and the Woods Hole Oceanographic Institution drew up plans to "catch" an ocean eddy. The result was the Mid-Ocean Dynamics Experiment (MODE).

After three years of preparation, MODE scientists went to sea in the spring of 1973. They "staked out" a 300-mile wide circle of ocean for close study. That circular area of ocean was located southwest of Bermuda—well within the Bermuda Triangle defined by Vincent Gaddis.

Six ships, three airplanes, and fifty oceanographers took part in the MODE study. Hundreds of instruments were placed on the surface of the ocean, at various depths, and on the ocean floor of the MODE study area. Information from these instruments enable MODE scientists to "catch" not one, but many different types of ocean eddies. An eddy with a warm water core and a swirling clockwise motion was tracked traveling westward through the study area. After it passed, another eddy appeared. It was moving eastward. It had a cold water core and a counterclockwise motion.

The MODE scientists discovered an enormous variety of eddies. They come in many different shapes, sizes, and energy levels. They can be found at almost any depth. Oceanographers found a great resemblance between eddies in the ocean and circular air movements in the atmosphere. They suspect that the two may be related. Air movements may greatly affect ocean movements, even at great depths, and ocean movements may affect air motions, even at great heights.

Project MODE didn't tell scientists how and why ocean eddies form. Neither did the scientists learn many details about how ocean eddies interact with the atmosphere and with ocean currents. Furthermore, no one knows whether ocean eddies can ever be a direct threat to ships or boats. Scientists are inclined to think that eddies are not a direct threat to surface vessels. However, they might trigger threatening atmospheric disturbances, and if deep-water eddies are part of undersea storms, they might be dangerous to submarines.

U.S. and Soviet scientists are planning another major program to study ocean eddies. The program will be conducted during 1977–78 in another circle of ocean southwest of Bermuda. The new program will be bigger than MODE. It will be called POLYMODE.

An eddy is a vortex in the ocean—a whirlpool. While oceanographers have been studying vortexes in the sea, meteorologists have been studying vortexes in the nearby sky. These vortexes in the sky are waterspouts. They frequently occur over the ocean area between Florida and Bermuda.

Unlike ocean eddies, waterspouts are not a new discovery. Columbus encountered them. So did countless sailors who sailed the seas after Columbus. But it wasn't until fairly recently that scientists tried to learn the nature of waterspouts.

Waterspouts resemble tornadoes. Some people call them "wet tornadoes." What's more, on rare occasions, tornadoes will move from the land over a patch of sea or lake and whip up water like a waterspout. But, in fact, waterspouts and tornadoes are produced by different atmospheric conditions. The weather conditions that spawn tornadoes do not occur over large bodies of water.

Waterspouts tend to form when the air over a patch of

Waterspouts often occur in the ocean area south and west of Bermuda. These funnels of spray whipped up from the sea surface are often called "wet tornados." Though they are not as powerful as tornados, waterspouts pose a threat to small ships, boats, and light airplanes. (*NOAA*)

ocean becomes very, very hot. This super-heating of the lower layer of air often happens in the ocean area between Florida and the Bahamas during the summer months. At that time, the sea surface is very warm, the air above it is hot and humid, and the trade winds are fairly calm.

Hot air rises. As it rises from above the sea surface, it lifts abundant moisture up into the cooler sections of the atmosphere. The result is a massive cloud system.

Hot air tends to spin as it rises. Sometimes a rising column of hot, moist air will spin fast enough to form a vortex or funnel reaching downward from the base of the cloud.

As the rising mass of water vapor cools and condenses, it gives off heat energy to the downward spiraling funnel. This added energy causes the funnel to spin faster. The faster it spins, the lower it reaches. Finally it touches the sea surface. Spray is whipped up into the funnel, and a waterspout is born.

Three waterspouts were seen at the same time in the Gulf of Mexico east of the Florida Straits. (*Exxon*)

A waterspout has a brief life—but a hectic one. It may last no more than 10 minutes. In that time, however, whirling winds in the waterspout can reach a speed of 150 miles per hour. That's enough to rip a boat, plane, or small ship apart.

Waterspouts can occur in all warm ocean areas. But they are a particular menace in the tropical Atlantic area bounded by Florida, Bermuda, and the West Indies.

Some people have wondered whether ocean eddies and waterspouts might be linked in some way. Could it be, they question, that warm moist air rising from over an eddy would have that "extra spin" needed to trigger the formation of a waterspout?

It is possible. But there is no evidence available at this time to show a connection between ocean eddies and waterspouts. If such a connection exists, however, weather scientists will surely find it.

World weather systems are now being studied as they have never been studied before. Scientists from many nations are taking part in a series of experiments to gain increased understanding of the atmosphere and of the causes of climatic variation and change. These experiments may continue into the next century. They are part of the Global Atmospheric Research Program, better known as GARP.

GARP is being conducted by the World Meteorological Organization and the International Council of Scientific Unions. United States participation in GARP is being coordinated by the National Oceanic and Atmospheric Administration (NOAA) of the U.S. Department of Commerce.

GARP experiments will hopefully provide the knowledge needed for long-range accurate weather prediction. The experiments may also tell us more about how weather systems affect life in various areas. Above all, the experiments may reveal the long-term effects of pollutants on the atmosphere. They may answer the question: Is the world getting warmer or colder?

Most GARP experiments will probe activities and phenomena in the layer of atmosphere just above the ocean surface. That is where global weather patterns are shaped.

Ocean water stores energy from the sun in the form of heat. Since the sun shines directly on the tropics throughout most of the year, the tropical regions of the world's oceans store a large proportion of the solar energy reaching the earth. Much of this energy is carried into the atmosphere as water evaporates. Then, as the water vapor cools and condenses in the atmosphere, the energy "explodes" in the form of weather. The resulting weather may be a raging hurricane or a cluster of gentle clouds floating lazily in the blue sky.

Vast quantities of heat and moisture are transferred from sea to air in the tropics. They are lifted high into the atmosphere by convective cloud systems. Then they spread throughout the global atmosphere.

The atmosphere has been called a giant heat engine whose

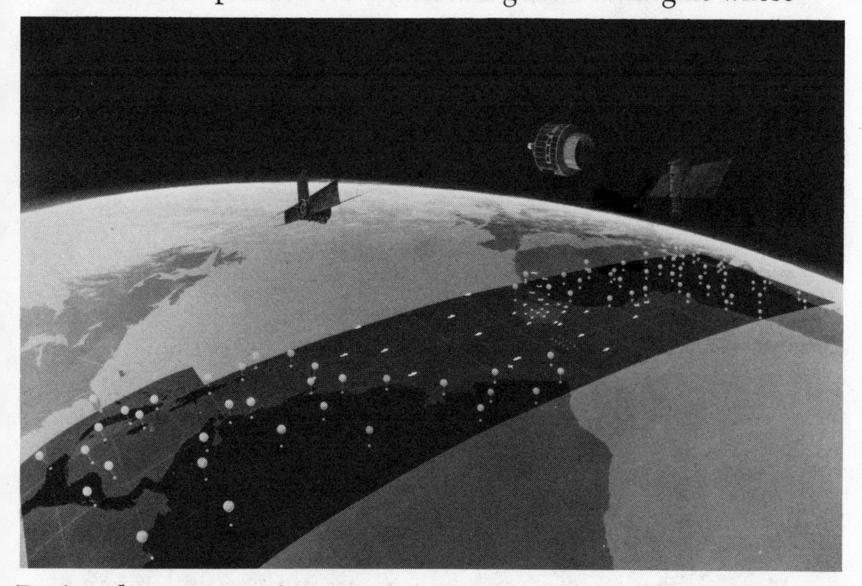

During the summer of 1974, scientists, ships, and aircraft from many nations engaged in an intensive study of the weather-making processes in the tropical region of the North Atlantic Ocean. The program was known as GATE (Global Atmospheric Research Program Atlantic Tropical Experiment). GATE scientists working on or near the ocean surface were greatly assisted by information from weather satellites orbiting overhead. (*NOAA*)

energy is provided by the sun's radiation. The tropical ocean region is the boilerroom of the world weather machine. Whatever happens in the boilerroom tends to affect the weather of the entire earth.

For that reason, GARP's first major experiment involved a very close study of the tropical atmosphere and ocean. This experiment was called GATE—GARP Atlantic Tropical Experiment. It lasted from June 15 to December 30, 1974. During that period, about 4000 scientists from 66 nations, 38 ships, 13 aircraft, and 6 satellites observed and measured conditions of the ocean and atmosphere ranging across the tropical Atlantic from Africa to the Americas.

During the period of intense study, nearly every cloud, gust of wind, and swirl of ocean current was tracked and measured. Satellites kept watch on the big weather picture in the area. At the same time, scientists in ships and planes examined all the slight variations of the sea and atmosphere. Flying at altitudes ranging from 300 to 30,000 feet, 13 airplanes from five nations probed a great variety of clouds. Special instruments on the planes measured temperatures, wind velocities and directions, moisture levels, and the amounts of tiny particles in and near the tropical cloud systems.

Balloons carried instruments high into the sky to measure wind velocities, air pressure, temperature, humidity, rainfall, and solar radiation. Radar, laser, and ultrasonic systems aboard the GATE fleet double checked the balloon-made measurements. Ship-borne instruments were also used to measure disturbances and dust layers in the lower atmosphere.

Though the atmosphere was much probed, the ocean was not neglected. Oceanographers and instruments on the ships measured sea temperatures, salinity, and current flows. Moored buoys were used to measure surface and internal ocean waves. Instruments on ships, planes, satellites, and buoys were used to study oceanic fronts. These fronts are lines where masses of cold and warm water meet and interact. They are similar to weather fronts in the atmosphere, where masses of cold and warm air meet. Many similarities and interactions between the oceanic and atmospheric systems were noted.

GATE experimenters provided masses of information. It will take scientists years to analyze and evaluate all the material. However, some information has already been processed and released. That information is giving scientists a clearer picture of the behavior of the tropical atmosphere and its effects on global weather.

Satellite pictures showed that clouds over the tropical ocean form in clusters. These cloud clusters are usually hundreds of miles wide. They tend to form at night. They usually move westward, and break up several days after they have formed. Clouds in the clusters may break up one by one. Therefore, a few clouds from a cluster may linger around for several days after the rest of the cluster has vanished.

Cloud clusters may lose or gain energy as they travel westward. Cloud clusters traveling westward from Africa across the Atlantic often gain energy as they go. When that happens, those cloud clusters tend to release much of their energy in the western tropical region of the Atlantic, southwest of Bermuda.

The cloud clusters of the tropics are in effect the steampipes from the tropical ocean boiler, pumping energy throughout the world weather machine. Cloud clusters lift energy from near the tropical ocean surface and take it high up into the atmosphere, beyond 40,000 feet. From there, the energy circulates throughout the global atmosphere.

In this system of cloud clusters, GATE experimenters discovered supernova storms. Scientists called them supernovas after the big, bright, explosive stage of a dying star.

These supernova storms are very different from normal

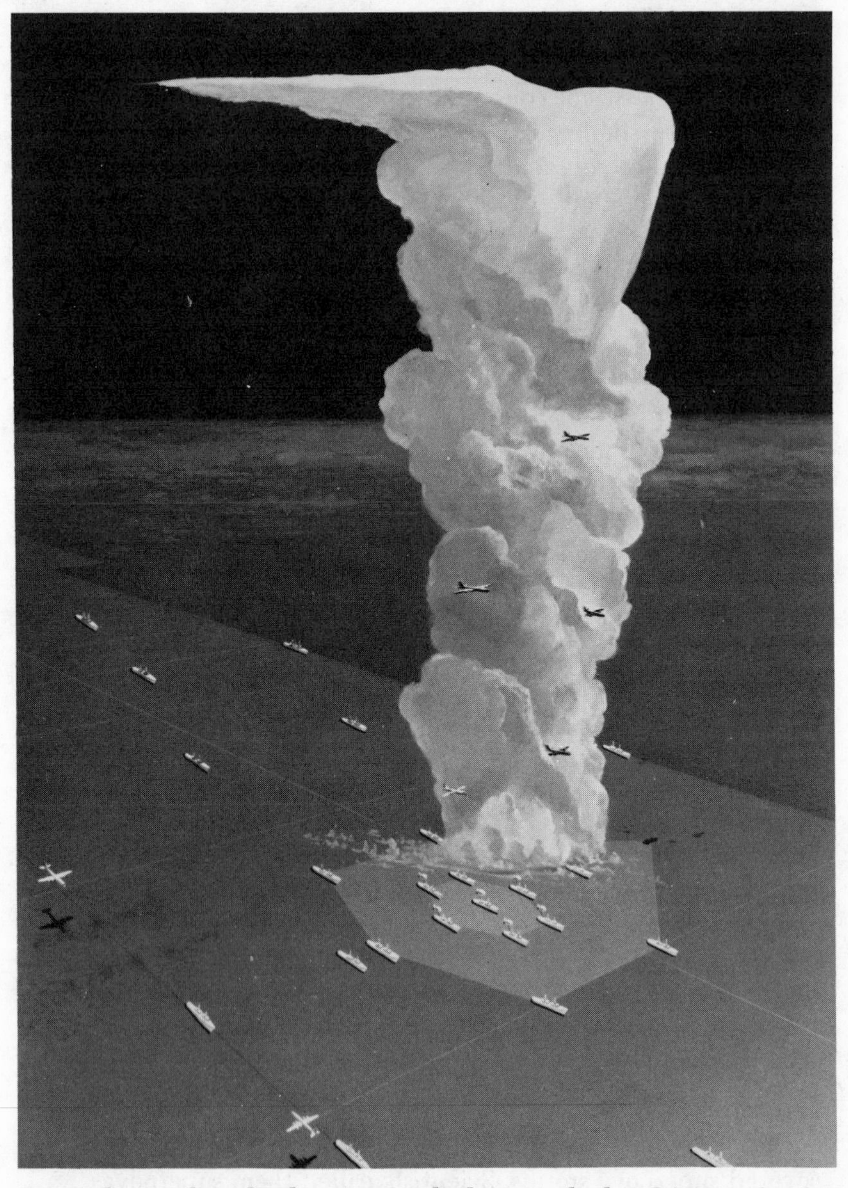

Tropical cumulus clouds were studied intensely by GATE scientists. (*NOAA*)

thunderstorms. Thunderstorms tend to develop in the daytime when sun-heated air lifts moisture high into the sky. But that's not the case with the supernova storms. They form only during the night over the ocean. Scientists don't know why they form at night. Dr. Helmut Weickmann of National Oceanic and Atmospheric Administration (NOAA) believes that the storms must come out of a strong atmospheric instability somewhere.

They grow rapidly, expanding from areas of a few hundred square miles to areas of thousands of square miles within an hour or two. Their growth is explosive, and their existence is violent. Fortunately, their existence is also brief. Supernova storms are born in the night and they tend to vanish with the morning light. They are definitely gone by noon the following day.

Supernova storms frequently develop over the eastern and central tropical regions of the Atlantic. They travel westward, and some of them may reach well into the western tropical region of the Atlantic before disappearing in daylight.

A plane flying over the tropical ocean at night could run into one of these sudden storms. By the time search planes could reach the area the next day, the plane and the storm would be gone. That brings us back to the question of unexplained ship and airplane disappearances in the western tropical region of the Atlantic.

Is there a mysterious Bermuda Triangle that swallows ships and planes?

The answer is NO!—if we're talking about a patch of ocean where uncanny forces are at work.

NO!—if we're talking about a place where space and time are all mixed up.

NO!—if we're talking about an *nth* dimension where ships, planes, and people are held suspended between life and death.

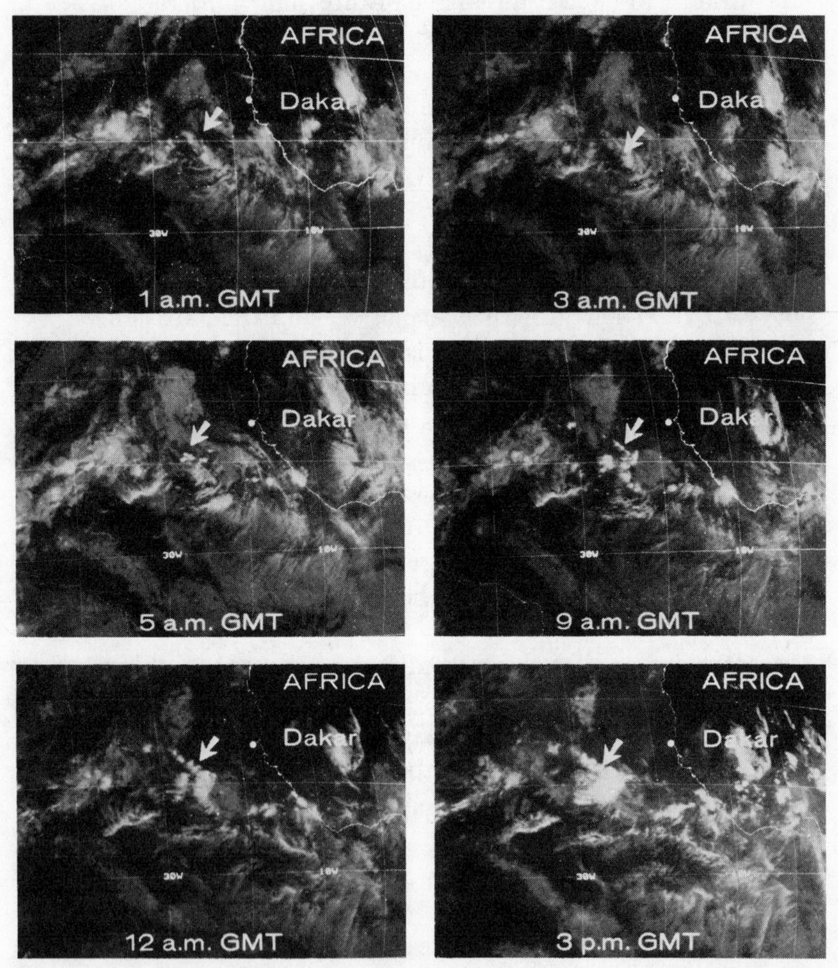

One of the great achievements of the GATE program was the discovery of "supernova" storms. These are storms that develop during the night off the west coast of Africa and swirl westward toward the Americas. Such storms last less than a day. Despite their short duration, these storms may have been responsible for many of the ship and plane losses of the Bermuda Triangle. (*NOAA*)

NO!—if we're talking about a place where invaders from another world have set up a base.

NO!—if we're talking about a sunken city where members of a lost civilization have left a killing machine.

But perhaps we mean a place were a mighty river of warm water forms and then rushes through the cool ocean. Perhaps we mean a place where swift currents hem in a seaweed sea. Perhaps we mean a place where energetic eddies swirl through the ocean. Perhaps we mean a place where whirling waterspouts link sea and sky in a few brief moment of fury. Perhaps we mean a place where young hurricanes come of age. Perhaps we mean a place where violent storms come and go in the night.

Perhaps we mean a place where ships and planes can be suddenly and unexpectedly overcome by the forces of nature. In that case, the answer is YES!

GATE ships at Dakar, West Africa, prepare to sweep across the ocean toward the West Indies in search of storms. (*NOAA*)

APPENDIX

SHIP AND AIRCRAFT LOSSES ASSOCIATED WITH THE BERMUDA TRIANGLE

Since the time of Christopher Columbus, thousands of ships have been lost in and around that mysterious patch of Atlantic Ocean known as the Bermuda Triangle. However, most of these losses are not mysterious. Many ships, particularly sailing ships, are known to have run aground on reefs, rocks, and sand bars in the vicinities of the Bahamas, Bermuda, the Carolina coast, and the Florida Keys. Old records tell the stories of these ship losses. In several cases wreckage of these lost ships has been found.

Many other ships are known to have been lost during storms and hurricanes in the area. Some ships burned at sea. Others capsized within sight of land. Still others are known to have been sunk by pirates and privateers.

However, a percentage of ship losses in that dangerous sea area cannot be specifically explained. As many as possible of those unexplained losses are listed here. Also listed here are ships and airplanes whose disappearances have been mentioned in the many books and articles that have been written about the Bermuda Triangle mystery.

Accounts of particular ship and plane disappearances in the Bermuda Triangle area often differ from book to book. This is particularly true of accounts of old sailing ship losses. Ship's names are not always spelled the same in each account. Conflicting dates and places are sometimes listed for certain losses.

In the following list of ship and airplane losses associated in some way with the Bermuda Triangle mystery, we've listed the most frequently used ships' names. We've also listed the most frequently used dates and places of the disappearances. Wherever major differences of opinion exist, we've noted those differences.

1495 *Gallega* and *Maria galante.* Ships in a fleet commanded by Christopher Columbus disappeared near the island of Hispaniola. The ships were probably lost in a hurricane.

1502 *El Dorado.* The flag ship of a treasure fleet that, along with seventeen other ships, was lost in the vicinity of Cuba.

1542 *San Miguel.* Spanish treasure ship that vanished near Hispaniola while enroute from Santo Domingo (Hispaniola) to Spain.

1579 *La Trinidad.* Spanish galleon lost somewhere near Jamaica while returning to Spain from the New World.

1609 *Sea Venture.* English ship taking colonists and supplies to Jamestown, Virginia, wrecked on the island of Bermuda. Survivors of the wreck under the command of Sir George Somers founded British colony of Bermuda. Though there was nothing mysterious about the loss of this ship, the loss was mentioned in at least two Bermuda Triangle mystery books.

1669 HMS *Port Royal.* According to old documents, this British warship was reported wrecked on the Bahama Island of Munsake. However, modern maps of the area do not show such an island.

1730 *Genvoese.* Ship of unknown nationality lost somewhere south of Jamaica.

1744 *Friendship.* English ship that disappeared while sailing from St. Kitts to Barbados in the West Indies.

1747 *Tryton.* Large English merchant ship that disappeared enroute from the Carolinas to England. The ship was presumed lost near Bermuda.

1748 *Industry.* English ship out of Boston, reported lost near Jamaica.

1753 *Griffin.* English merchant ship lost near Cuba while en route from Jamaica to England. In some accounts the name of this ship is listed as *Griffen.*

1757 *Mary.* English ship that disappeared somewhere between Antigua in the West Indies and Philadelphia, Pennsylvania. Many ships named *Mary* have been listed lost in the Bermuda Triangle area at various times.

1763 *Patty.* English merchant ship lost while en route from England to Bahamas.

1763 *Alexander.* English ship lost near Florida while en route from Jamaica to England.

1777 HMS *Repulse.* English warship that disappeared in the vicinity of Bermuda. According to some reports, the big ship turned over in a gale.

1780 HMS *Phoenix.* The loss of this English warship was not a mystery—it went down in a storm and some survivors and papers were retrieved. However, a description of the storm provided a note of mystery. A ship's officer wrote that the "sea was on fire."

1799 *Minerva.* U.S. merchant ship that disappeared somewhere off the coast of Georgia.

1800 USS *Insurgent.* This United States warship disappeared in the Caribbean. Very little is known about this ship or the circumstances of the loss.

1800 USS *Pickering.* A United States frigate with a crew of ninety disappeared while en route from New Castle, Delaware, to Guadeloupe in the West Indies.

1803 *Margaret.* A United States merchant ship that disappeared between Virginia and Barbados.

1804 *Catherine.* British ship lost, probably in the Gulf of

Mexico or the Florida Straits, while en route from New Orleans, Louisiana, to England.

1805 *Ocean.* British merchant ship lost near the Virgin Islands while en route from the West Indies to England.

1812 *Patriot.* A United States ship with the daughter of Aaron Burr aboard that disappeared while en route from Charleston (Georgetown in some accounts), South Carolina, to New York. Some old accounts say that the ship was attacked by pirates. An old painting even shows Burr's daughter, Theodosia Alston, fighting off pirates as they try to board the *Patriot.* But there is no evidence to support this theory. If pirates had captured or killed such a famous woman, it is doubtful that the fact would have remained a secret.

1813 HMS *Subtle.* British warship that disappeared somewhere among the West Indies. The ship could have fallen victim to American or French warships.

1814 USS *Wasp.* Large United States warship with a crew of 140 that was last seen in the Caribbean. According to one account, the warship was lost off the coast of South Carolina. Though no explanation can be given for the disappearance of the USS *Wasp,* the ship was lost during a time of war.

1814 *Metcalf.* British merchant ship that disappeared while en route from Jamaica to England.

1817 *Arabella.* A United States merchant ship believed to have been lost in the vicinity of the Virgin Islands while en route from Brazil to New York.

1818 *Nautilus.* German ship lost somewhere in the vicinity of Puerto Rico.

1822 *Actif.* French merchant ship that disappeared while en route from Havana, Cuba, to Le Havre, France. The ship was presumed lost in the vicinity of Cuba.

1824 USS *Wild Cat* (spelled Wildcat in some accounts). Small United States naval vessel said to have disappeared while sailing from Cuba to Thompson's Island, Boston.

1824 *Rosalie.* Several writers say that a French sailing ship named *Rosalie* was lost en route to Havana, Cuba. Some accounts claim that the vessel was found abandoned in the Bermuda Triangle area. The vessel was said to have been in shipshape condition and its only occupant was a half-starved canary in a cage. In *The Bermuda Triangle Mystery—Solved,* Lawrence Kusche states that he could find no record of such an incident or of such a ship. He did, however, find a notice that a ship named *Rossini* or *Rosini* was lost around that time.

1843 USS *Grampus.* A veteran United States warship vanished while returning to Charleston, South Carolina, from a West Indies patrol. The warship was last sighted sailing northward off the Florida coast on March 3, 1843.

1854 *Bella.* According to some accounts, a schooner was found floating in the West Indies. The vessel was said to have been in perfect condition, but there was no sign of the crew and no indication of why they would have abandoned ship. Lawrence Kusche claims that the *Bella* itself was not found. He says that debris, some of it marked *Bella,* was found off the coast of Brazil, hundred of miles south of the Bermuda Triangle.

1854 *City of Glasgow.* British ocean liner with 399 passengers and 81 crewmen vanished while en route from Liverpool to Philadelphia.

1855 *James B. Chester.* American three-masted sailing ship, said to have been found drifting crewless in the Sargasso Sea. According to most accounts, the ship's boats were in place and the cargo was untouched. Some accounts also say that the ship's main cabin was in disarray and that the ship's compass and papers were missing.

1866 *Lotta.* Swedish bark said to have disappeared while en route from Göteborg, Sweden, to Havana, Cuba.

1868 *Viego.* Spanish sailing ship said to have disappeared between Spain and Cuba.

1872 *Mary Celeste* (sometimes misspelled as *Marie Celeste*). One hundred and three-foot-long brigantine, found floating intact but crewless in the Atlantic Ocean east of the Azores. There was no indication as to why the ship was abandoned. Though the mystery of the *Mary Celeste* is mentioned in most Bermuda Triangle books, the deserted ship was actually found more than a thousand miles from the Bermuda Triangle.

1880 HMS *Atalanta.* British training frigate with about 280 persons aboard sailed out of Hamilton Harbor, Bermuda, bound for Britain, on January 31, 1880. The ship was never seen again.

1881 Unidentified schooner was said to have been found floating in the Atlantic Ocean west of the Azores by the crew of the brig, *Ellen Austin.*

1881 *Miramon.* Italian schooner said to have disappeared while en route from Cuba to New Orleans, Louisiana.

1902 *Freya.* German bark which, according to some accounts, was lost while en route from Manzanillo, Cuba, to Chile. The ship was later found crewless. Lawrence Kusche shows that the ship was actually en route from Manzanillo on the west coast of Mexico to Chile, and that the ship was found crewless off Mazatlán, also off the west coast of Mexico. The tragedy of the *Freya* occurred in the Pacific Ocean.

1909 *Spray.* A 36-foot yawl manned by Joshua Slocum, the first person to sail around the world alone, disappeared while en route from Martha's Vineyard, Massachusetts, to the Orinoco River in South America. Some accounts say that the *Spray* visited Miami before the yawl and its famous crewman disappeared.

1910 USS *Nina*. This United States Navy ocean-going tug disappeared while sailing from Norfolk, Virginia, to Havana, Cuba. The tug was reportedly last sighted off Savannah, Georgia.

1918 USS *Cyclops*. This Navy collier disappeared with 309 men aboard while en route from Brazil to Baltimore, Maryland. Some accounts say that the ship's destination was Norfolk, Virgina. The USS *Cyclops* was last sighted steaming north from Barbados.

1920 *Allyan* (in some accounts *Albyan*). Russian bark that disappeared after sailing out of Norfolk, Virginia.

1920 *Yute*. Spanish steamship that disappeared while en route from Baltimore, Maryland, to Europe. An SOS call from the ship gave its position as 240 miles southeast of Cape May, New Jersey. Rescue ships rushed to that area, but no trace of the steamship could be found.

1920 *Flonine*. Norwegian bark that disappeared after sailing out of Hampton Roads, Virginia. In some accounts, this ship is called *Florino*.

1920 *William O'Brien*. American merchant ship that disappeared while en route from New York to Rotterdam. A radio message from the ship indicated difficulties at a position about 500 miles east of Delaware. No trace of the ship was found.

1920 *General Morne*. This British schooner vanished while en route from Lisbon, Portugal, to Newfoundland.

1921 *Carroll A. Deering*. Five-masted schooner that went aground on Diamond Shoals, Virginia. When rescuers reached the vessel, no trace of the crew could be found.

1921 *Hewitt*. American steamship out of Portland, Maine, that disappeared in the Atlantic. The *Hewitt* was said to have been off Diamond Shoals around the same time as the *Carroll A. Deering*. It was suggested that the *Hewitt* had picked up the crew of the *Carroll A. Deer-*

ing. But there is no evidence to support that suggestion.

1921 *Esparanza de Larrinaga*. Schooner said to have disappeared after sailing out of Norfolk, Virginia.

1921 *Monte San Michele*. This Italian steamship disappeared while en route from Baltimore, Maryland, to Europe.

1921 *Ottawa*. British tanker reported lost off the east coast of the United States, probably in the Virginia area.

1921 *Swartskog* (also spelled *Svartskog*). Norwegian bark that disappeared off U.S. east coast.

1921 *Canadian Maid*. British schooner that disappeared while en route from Italy to New York.

1921 *Steinsund*. This Norwegian bark disappeared off the east coast of the U.S.

1925 *Raifuku Maru*. Japanese steamship that was lost while enroute from Boston, Massachusetts, to Hamburg, Germany. According to the *Dictionary of Disasters at Sea in the Age of Steam,* the ship sent out an SOS from a position 400 miles east of Boston. By this account, the final message from the ship was, "Now very danger, come quick." The liner *Homeric* rushed to the rescue. But high seas prevented the crew of the Homeric from taking off the crew of the *Raifuku Maru,* and the Japanese ship was seen to go down with all hands. According to several Bermuda Triangle mystery books, the fate of the *Raifuku Maru* was unknown, and the final message from the ship was, "Danger like dagger. Come quick."

1925 *Cotopaxi*. A large cargo ship that disappeared while en route from Charleston, South Carolina, to Havana, Cuba. A fierce gale was reported in the western Atlantic region around the time of the disappearance.

1926 *Porta Noca*. Small passenger ship that disappeared between the Isle of Pines and mainland Cuba.

1926 *Suduffco*. Cargo ship with a crew of twenty-nine men

that sailed from Port Newark, New Jersey, for the Panama Canal and eventually Los Angeles. The ship never reached the Panama Canal. No trace of it was ever found. Several storms were reported in the western Atlantic around the time of the *Suduffco*'s last voyage.

1928 *Vestris.* Liner that disappeared while en route to Barbados.

1931 Light plane piloted by Herbie Pond, a noted rum runner, disappeared while returning to the Bahamas after having delivered a load of whiskey to West Palm Beach, Florida.

1931 *Stavanger* (or *Stavenger*). Norwegian freighter with forty-three persons aboard was said to have disappeared among the Bahama Islands. Though the loss of this ship has been mentioned in most Bermuda Triangle books, Lawrence Kusche could find no newspaper reports or official records of the loss. In fact, he could find no record of the ship's existence.

1932 *John and Mary.* An American yacht found drifting crewless about fifty miles south of Bermuda.

1935 *La Dahama.* Yacht whose crew was rescued by the Italian liner *Rex.* People aboard the *Rex* claimed to have seen *La Dahama* sink, yet the crews of two other ships claim to have boarded *La Dahama* at a later date.

1935 A four-passenger airplane was said to have disappeared while flying from Havana to the Isle of Pines, Cuba.

1938 *Anglo-Australian.* British freighter with a crew of thirty-nine was said to have disappeared southwest of the Azores.

1940 *Gloria Colite* (also spelled *Gloria Colita* in some accounts). A schooner from St. Vincent, British West Indies, was found drifting crewless 200 miles south of Mobile, Alabama. The ship had been taking a cargo of lumber from Mobile to Guantanamo, Cuba. The fate of the crew was never learned. However, the schooner appeared to have been battered by a storm.

1941 *Proteus.* American collier that disappeared while en route from St. Thomas, Virgin Islands, to Portland, Maine.

1941 *Nereus.* This sister ship of the *Proteus* also disappeared while en route from St. Thomas to Portland. The two ships were sailing a few days apart around the time the United States entered World War II. It is possible that both coal ships were sunk by German submarines.

1941 *Mahukona.* Freighter that disappeared while en route from Norfolk, Virginia, to Brazil. An SOS from the ship gave its last position as 600 miles east of Jacksonville, Florida. No trace of the vessel was found.

1944 *Rubicon.* Cuban freighter found drifting off the east coast of Florida. Coast Guardsmen who boarded the vessel found only a dog aboard. No trace of the crew was found. Because a broken piece of rope that might have been used to moor the ship to a dock was found on the ship's bow, it was suggested at the time that the ship's crew may have gone ashore, and the rope holding the ship to the dock may have snapped. However, the ship's lifeboats were missing. That would suggest abandonment at sea.

1944 Seven U.S. bomber aircraft en route from Florida to Italy made a stopover in Bermuda. Shortly after continuing the flight, two planes returned to Bermuda. Their crews complained of severe air turbulence. The other five planes disappeared.

1945 Five Navy torpedo bomber aircraft constituting Training Flight 19 disappeared during a mission out over the Atlantic Ocean from Fort Lauderdale, Florida.

1945 A PBM flying boat patrol plane disappeared while searching for Flight 19.

1945 *Voyager II.* A 70-foot schooner with four persons aboard disappeared somewhere off the coast of Virginia or the Carolinas.

1945 *Valmore.* Two-masted schooner that disappeared off the coast of North Carolina.

1946 *City Belle.* A schooner out of Nassau, in the Bahamas, was found deserted at sea. A Nassau newspaper later reported that seven crew members of the *City Belle* were rescued from an open boat.

1947 A C-54 cargo airplane was said to have disappeared about 100 miles east of Bermuda. In some accounts this airplane is said to have been a B-29 or B-50 Superfortress bomber. Various conflicting accounts of the place and time of the disappearance have been given.

1948 *Star Tiger.* A Tudor IV airliner of British South American Airways bound for Bermuda disappeared after the pilot had reported the plane's position as 400 miles northeast of Bermuda.

1948 Small boat containing jockey Al Snider (spelled Snyder in some accounts) disappeared off the Florida Keys. Gale was reported in the area around the time of the loss. The battered boat was eventually found but no trace of the three men was ever discovered.

1948 DC-3 chartered airliner disappeared on a flight from Puerto Rico to Miami, Florida. Thirty-five persons were aboard.

1949 *Star Ariel.* A Tudor IV airliner, sister ship to *Star Tiger,* disappeared between Bermuda and Jamaica.

1949 *Driftwood.* A fishing boat with five persons aboard disappeared between Fort Lauderdale, Florida, and Bimini in the Bahamas.

1950 *Sandra.* Small freighter that disappeared while en route from Savannah, Georgia, to Puerto Cabello, Venezuela.

1950 DC-3 airliner with missionaries aboard disappeared

somewhere between Miami, Florida, and Venezuela.

1951 *São Paulo.* Ocean liner bound for scrapping broke away from tugs that were towing the ship southwest of the Azores. The ocean liner and a caretaker crew of eight men disappeared.

1953 British York aircraft on a flight to Jamaica disappeared after sending out an SOS signal that ended abruptly. According to some accounts, this plane disappeared between the Azores and Newfoundland.

1954 A U.S. Navy super-constellation aircraft with forty-two persons aboard disappeared during a flight from New Jersey to the Azores.

1954 *Southern Districts.* A freighter with a load of sulphur disappeared while sailing from Louisiana to Maine. By some accounts, the ship was lost in the Florida Straits. By other accounts, the ship was said to have been sighted off Charleston, South Carolina, and therefore must have been lost north of that point.

1955 *Home Sweet Home.* This schooner vanished while sailing from Bermuda to Antigua in the West Indies.

1955 *Connemara IV.* A yacht found crewless about 150 miles southeast of Bermuda. A hurricane had passed near the area where the yacht was found a few days earlier.

1956 A B-25 bomber converted to carry cargo was lost southeast of Florida.

1956 A PBM Navy patrol seaplane disappeared on a mission out of Bermuda. The plane's last reported position was 352 miles north of Bermuda. The crew of a freighter some distance from that area reported a "plane overhead in flames" at roughly the time of the seaplane's disappearance.

1958 *Revonoc.* Racing yacht owned and manned by millionaire publisher Harvey Conover disappeared while sailing from Key West to Miami. Strong gales were reported in the area at the time.

1962 USAF KB-50 tanker aircraft disappeared on a flight from Virginia to the Azores.

1963 Two USAF KC-135 tanker aircraft vanished during a refueling mission out of Homestead AFB, Florida. A midair collision of the two aircraft was strongly suspected but not proven.

1963 *Marine Sulphur Queen.* Tanker carrying sulphur disappeared while sailing from Beaumont, Texas, to Norfolk, Virginia.

1963 *Sno' Boy.* Fishing boat that disappeared between Kingston and Northeast Cay, eighty miles southwest of Jamaica.

1963 C-132 transport aircraft lost over the Atlantic while en route to the Azores.

1964 *Enchantress.* This yacht disappeared after sailing out of Charleston, South Carolina, bound for the Panama Canal. A radio call from the vessel reported trouble off the Florida coast. No trace of the yacht was found.

1964 *Crystal.* Yacht that disappeared after sailing out from Fort George, Florida. Four years later, the waterlogged hulk of the yacht was found drifting 150 miles east of Jacksonville, Fla.

1965 C-119 Air Force transport plane with ten men aboard disappeared on a flight from Homestead Air Force Base, Florida, to Grand Turk in the Bahamas.

1965 *El Gato.* A houseboat that disappeared while sailing from Great Inagua to Grand Turk in the Bahamas.

1967 YC-122 converted cargo airplane used to film movies disappeared while flying from Palm Beach, Florida, to Grand Bahama Island.

1967 Light airplane disappeared on a flight out from Key Largo, Florida.

1967 Light airplane piloted by Phil Quigley disappeared while en route from Cozumel, Mexico, to Honduras.

1967 Piper Apache light airplane disappeared on a flight

from San Juan, Puerto Rico, to St. Thomas, Virgin Islands.

1967 Light airplane with two doctors and their wives aboard is said to have disappeared on a flight from Jamaica to Nassau in the Bahamas.

1967 Light airplane piloted by Hector Guzman disappeared on a flight from Fort Lauderdale, Florida, to San Juan, Puerto Rico.

1967 *Witchcraft.* Cabin cruiser that sailed a short distance out from Miami and disappeared. Gale-force winds were reported at the time.

1968 USS *Scorpion.* Nuclear-powered submarine that sank for some unknown reason west of the Azores. Wreckage of the submarine was located and photographed on the deep ocean floor.

1968 *Ithaca Island.* The freighter disappeared en route from Norfolk, Virginia, to Liverpool, England.

1969 Light airplane piloted by Caroline Coscio disappeared on a flight from Pompano Beach, Florida, to Jamaica.

1969 Twin-engined Beechcraft airplane said to have disappeared on a flight from Jamaica to Nassau, Bahamas.

1969 *Vagabond.* Sloop found deserted and drifting in the western region of the Atlantic. Peter Wallin of Sweden had been sailing the craft to Australia.

1969 *Teignmouth Electron.* Yacht which was being sailed around the world by Donald Crowhurst was found drifting crewless in the Atlantic. There was some speculation at the time that the yacht's only crewman, Mr. Crowhurst, may have committed suicide by stepping overboard. But there was no evidence to support that conclusion.

1969 *Brendan the Bold.* This yacht disappeared about 400 miles northeast of Puerto Rico. The vessel was being sailed by Capt. Bill Verity, who in 1966 had crossed the Atlantic alone in a small boat. It was later reported that Verity had survived.

1969 *Southern Cross.* Yacht found drifting crewless off Cape May, New Jersey.

1970 *Milton Iatrides.* Freighter that disappeared while sailing from New Orleans, Louisiana, to Cape Town, South Africa.

1971 *Elizabeth.* A freighter that disappeared while en route from Port Everglades, Florida, to Venezuela. The ship was said to have been last sighted in the Windward Passage between Haiti and Cuba.

1971 F-4 Phantom jet fighter plane vanished on a flight out to sea from Homestead Air Force Base, Florida. The plane was tracked by radar to a point about eighty-five miles southeast of Miami.

1971 *Caribe.* Motor ship that vanished while en route from Colombia, South America, to the Dominican Republic.

1971 *Ixtapa.* This cabin cruiser vanished while traveling from Cozumel, Mexico, to the Florida Keys.

1971 *Lucky Edur.* Fishing boat found drifting deserted in the Atlantic, south of the New Jersey coast.

1973 *Anita.* Norwegian freighter that disappeared while carrying a cargo of coal from Norfolk, Virginia, to Hamburg, Germany.

1973 *Norse Variant.* Sister ship to *Anita.* Left Norfolk almost at the same time with a cargo of coal for Hamburg. About 150 miles southeast of Cape May, New Jersey, the *Norse Variant* radioed that the ship was foundering in stormy seas. Three days later, a sole survivor of the *Norse Variant* was rescued, and he described how the freighter was lost in a fierce storm. It was then assumed that the *Anita* was a victim of the same storm.

1973 Beechcraft Bonanza airplane disappeared on a flight from Fort Lauderdale, Florida, to Grand Abaco Island in the Bahamas.

1973 Navion 16 light airplane disappeared on a flight from West Palm Beach, Florida, to Freeport, Bahamas.

1974 *Saba Bank.* Yacht that vanished while sailing from Nassau, Bahamas, to Miami, Florida.

SUGGESTED FURTHER READINGS

Berlitz, Charles. *The Bermuda Triangle.* New York: Doubleday & Co., 1974.

Berman, Bruce D. *Encyclopedia of American Shipwrecks.* Boston: Mariners Press, 1972.

Briggs, Peter. *Men In The Sea.* New York: Simon & Schuster, 1968.

Brown, Raymond Lamont. *Phantoms of the Sea.* New York: Taplinger Publishing Co., 1973.

Burgess, Robert F. *Sinkings, Salvages, Shipwrecks.* New York: American Heritage Press, 1970.

Carter, Samuel III. *The Gulf Stream Story.* New York: Doubleday & Co., 1970.

Ebon, Martin, ed. *The Riddle of the Bermuda Triangle.* New York: New American Library, 1975.

Edwards, Frank. *Stranger Than Science.* New York: Lyle Stuart, 1959.

Freuchen, Peter. *Peter Freuchen's Book of The Seven Seas.* New York: Simon & Schuster, 1957.

Gaddis, Vincent. *Invisible Horizons.* Philadelphia: Chilton, 1965.

Godwin, John. *This Baffling World.* New York: Hart Publishing Co., 1968.

Gould, Rupert. *Enigmas.* New Hyde Park, N. Y.: University Books, 1965.

Hoehling, A. A. *They Sailed Into Oblivion.* New York: Thomas Yoseloff Co., 1958.

Horner, David. *The Treasure Galleons.* New York: Dodd, Mead & Co., 1971.

Jacobs, Francine. *The Sargasso Sea—An Ocean Desert.* New York: William Morrow, 1975.

Jeffrey, Adi-Kent Thomas. *The Bermuda Triangle.* New York: Warner Paperback Library, 1975.

Jennings, Gary. *The Killer Storms.* Philadelphia: J. P. Lippincott Co., 1970.

Kusche, Lawrence David. *The Bermuda Triangle Mystery—Solved.* New York: Harper & Row, 1975.

Landsburg, Alan, and Landsburg, Sally. *In Search of Ancient Mysteries.* New York: Bantam Books, 1974.

Marx, Robert F. *Shipwrecks of the Western Hemisphere.* New York: World Publishing Co., 1971.

Morison, Samuel Eliot. *Christopher Columbus, Mariner.* Boston: Little Brown & Co., 1955.

Nichols, Elizabeth. *The Devil's Sea.* New York: Award Books, 1975.

Sanderson, Ivan T. *Invisible Residents.* New York: T. Y. Crowell, 1970.

Smith, F. G. Walton. *The Seas In Motion.* New York: T. Y. Crowell, 1973.

Smith, Warren. *Triangle of the Lost.* New York: Zebra Books, 1975.

Snow, Edward Rowe. *Mysteries and Adventures Along the Atlantic Coast.* New York: Dodd, Mead & Co., 1948.

———. *Unsolved Mysteries of Sea and Shore.* New York: Dodd, Mead & Co., 1963.

Spencer, John Wallace. *Limbo of the Lost.* New York: Bantam Books, 1973.

———. *No Earthly Explanation.* Westfield, Mass.: Phillips, 1974.

Stewart, Oliver. *Danger In The Air.* New York: Philosophical Library, 1958.

Stommell, H. *The Gulf Stream: A Physical Dynamical Description.* Berkeley: University of California Press, 1965.

Teal, John, and Teal, Mildred. *The Sargasso Sea.* Boston: Little Brown & Co., 1975.

Titler, Dale. *Wings of Mystery.* New York: Dodd, Mead & Co., 1966.

Villiers, Alan. *Posted Missing.* New York: Charles Scribner's Sons, 1974.

———. *Wild Ocean.* New York: Charles Scribner's Sons, 1957.

Weiss, Malcolm. *Storms From The Inside Out.* New York: Julian Messner, 1973.

Winer, Richard. *The Devil's Triangle.* New York: Bantam Books, 1974.

INDEX

ABOUT THE AUTHOR

Michael J. Cusack was born in Cork, Ireland. He attended Columbia University and Fairleigh Dickinson University. He is presently an associate editor at *Science World*, Scholastic Magazines Inc.

Mr. Cusack has written many articles on science, many of which have received writing awards. He has on numerous occasions received the Educational Press Association of America Distinguished Achievement Award.

Mr. Cusack and his wife, Anne, live in Englewood, New Jersey, with their three daughters, Deborah, Deirdre, and Jennifer.